STARTING YOUR OWN BUSINESS

FOURTH EDITION

Ron Immink & Brian O'Kane

Downloads and additional information available @
www.startingabusinessinireland.com

Published by OAK TREE PRESS
www.oaktreepress.com / www.SuccessStore.com
www.startingabusinessinireland.com

© 1997; 2001; 2009, 2018 Minister for Business, Enterprise and Innovation.

ISBN 978-1-78119-300-6 Paperback
ISBN 978-1-78119-301-3 ePub
ISBN 978-1-78119-302-0 Kindle
ISBN 978-1-78119-303-7 PDF

Printed in Ireland by SPRINTPrint.

Acknowledgements
Production of first edition of this guide in 1997 was assisted by the European
Commission through the Community SME Initiative under Measure 4 of the
Small Business Operational Programme.
The authors gratefully acknowledge the assistance they received from the
organisations mentioned in this guide, the staff of the Department and the many
others who have contributed to the research for this and earlier editions.

Disclaimer
The contents of this guide are believed to be correct at the time of printing but no
responsibility can be taken by the authors, the publisher or the Department of
Business, Enterprise and Innovation for any errors herein. Readers should take
professional advice before entering into any legally binding commitments or
investing any funds.

CONTENTS

READY?

Introduction 4
What Makes an Entrepreneur? 5
Self-assessment 7
Developing Your Idea 10
Identifying Future Trends 13
Market Research 15
Business Model Canvas 20
Testing Your Idea 21
Training for Entrepreneurs 23
Start-up Alternatives 25

STEADY

Introduction 32
Developing a Strategy 33
Innovation 37
Competitiveness 39
Marketing 41
Products & Production 61
Staff 63
Which Legal Structure? 75
Business Names 79
Bank Accounts 81
Taxation 82
Accounting 91
Insurance 98
Trading Laws 100
Premises 102
Finance 105

Financial Projections 116
Cashflow Planning 124
Sources of Assistance 129
Reducing Risk 131
Mentors 133
Professional Advisers 135
Your Business Plan 137
Pitching your Plan 160
Smell the Flowers 163

GO!

Introduction 166
Completing the Accounts Pages 167
Job Application 170
Job Description 171
Employment Contract 172
Safety Statement 175
Quality 176
Environmental Concerns 179
Health and Safety 181
Intellectual Property 183
Cyber-security 186
Monitoring Performance 187

APPENDIX

Sources of Assistance 189

INTRODUCTION

The harsh reality is that too many new businesses fail – many more than ought to. Why? Because of lack of planning. They do not plan to fail, but they fail to plan.

Preparation – in the form of careful and considered planning – is the most important thing you can do to ensure that your fledgling business gets off the ground and continues flying. You can never eliminate all risk but you can reduce it significantly – to the point where the odds are in your favour.

This workbook is all about preparation – preparing you for what you will face as an entrepreneur, for the obstacles, hurdles and blockages that will be placed in your way, for the new skills that you will have to learn, for the tasks that you will have to handle, for the rules, regulations and form-filling that may trip you up, right through to the agencies – State and private sector – that can help you make your dream a success.

The first edition of this workbook was developed in 1997 for the then Department of Enterprise, Trade & Employment under Measure 4 of the Government's Operational Programme for Small Business, which was funded by the European Commission. Twenty years on, this is now the fourth edition of what has become *the* text on business planning for start-ups in Ireland.

This edition incorporates all the best and latest thinking on business planning, including the Business Model Canvas and other techniques. However, we feel that the READY – STEADY – GO! format is still the most valid structure, particularly for less experienced entrepreneurs. Compared to 20 years ago, the emphasis is now more on early proof that your business is going to work, including a heavier emphasis on (early) sales – that is simply due to the speed-up in business life cycles. Twenty years ago, it was more difficult to start a business – but easier to stay in business. Now it's the opposite – now, to stay in business, you need to be hypercompetitive from the word 'Go'.

STARTING YOUR OWN BUSINESS: A Workbook was designed to take a potential entrepreneur through the whole process of starting a business, from first thoughts about self-employment to the practicalities of start-up.

The workbook consists of three core chapters:

- **READY:** The first chapter, covering preparation, self-assessment, ideas generation, market research and training for entrepreneurs
- **STEADY:** The bulk of the guide, covering business planning, raising finance, sources of assistance, choosing premises, recruiting staff, marketing, book-keeping and management issues

1

- **GO!:** When everything has been thought through and you are ready, this section provides the remaining information you need to get started and keep your business going strong.

As you work through this workbook, you will find checklists, flowcharts and questionnaires designed to make you think about your proposed business. The aim is not only to give you the theory behind setting up a business but also to give you the practical tools to actually do it. It all adds up to a turn-key package – almost a 'business in a box'.

Each chapter in this workbook is introduced by KEY QUESTIONS – searching questions that you, as a potential entrepreneur, need to consider carefully before moving ahead. Before you read the chapter, think through your answers to these key questions (but do not write down those answers yet). When you have completed the chapter, have read all the sections and have worked through all the checklists and questionnaires, you should then come back to the key questions and complete your answers in writing.

In each section of the workbook, you will find clearly-stated OBJECTIVES set out beside the section heading. These summarise what you can expect to learn from the section.

Read them before you begin, to decide whether the section is relevant to your needs. And when you have finished the section, go back, read the objectives again and check them off.

When you have reached the end of the workbook, use the answers to the questions to complete your business plan. And then, when you have done that and filled in and sent out all the forms that are necessary, your funding is in place – it's time to rock and roll!

To help you even more, this workbook is supported by a website, **www.startingabusinessinireland.com**, where you will find spreadsheets and templates to download, as well as updated and additional information and resources.

Good luck.

Ron Immink, Dublin / Spain
Brian O'Kane, Cork
December 2017

PS: And if you have any suggestions on how to improve this workbook, feel free to send us an email to **info@oaktreepress.com**.

READY

KEY QUESTIONS

Do you have the skills / experience needed to run a business?

☐ YES ☐ NO

Do you have sufficient motivation to stick with it for as long as it takes?

☐ YES ☐ NO

Do you have the support of your family? ☐ YES ☐ NO

Does your business idea appear to test out? ☐ YES ☐ NO

Are you aware of the financial implications of self-employment?

☐ YES ☐ NO

Is your business:

> A start-up? ☐ YES ☐ NO

> Buy-in of an existing business? ☐ YES ☐ NO

> Franchise? ☐ YES ☐ NO

> Network marketing? ☐ YES ☐ NO

Do you need further training? ☐ YES ☐ NO

Are you ready for the next step – researching in more detail before you write your business plan? ☐ YES ☐ NO

These Key Questions are designed to focus your thoughts as you read this chapter. Think through your answers before you start to read the chapter. Then come back and write down your answers before moving on to the next chapter.

INTRODUCTION

Almost 70% of people who become self-employed do not prepare themselves properly for their new role and responsibilities:

- Specifically, almost 90% do not study their market
- As a result, on average about 50% of all businesses in Europe fail within five years of starting.

These statistics should show you the importance of preparation and of carefully considering whether entrepreneurship is right for you – though you should also balance this with Paul Dickson's quote in the page margin.

Chapter structure

This chapter takes you through:

- What makes an entrepreneur?
- Self-assessment (including assessment of your business partners)
- Developing your idea
- Identifying future trends
- Market research
- Business model canvas
- Testing your idea
- Training for entrepreneurs
- Start-up alternatives.

Key Questions

The Key Questions on the previous page are designed to focus your thoughts as you read this chapter. Think through your answers to these questions before you start to read the chapter. Then come back and write down your answers before moving on to the next chapter.

Ignore all the statistics that tell you that 95% of all new businesses fail in the first eight years. Not only are these 'statistics' riddled with widely wrong assumptions and false failure rates, but they don't apply to you. Dwelling on the statistics is like staying up to study divorce rates on your wedding night.
PAUL DICKSON

Whatever you think it's gonna take, double it. That applies to money, time, stress. It's gonna be harder than you think and take longer than you think.
RICHARD A CORTESE, on starting a business

WHAT MAKES AN ENTREPRENEUR?

Entrepreneurship is the dynamic process of creating wealth, undertaken by people who assume a risk in terms of money, energy, time and / or career commitment of creating value through the provision of some product or service. The product or service may or may not be new or unique but value somehow must be created by the entrepreneur by securing and using the necessary skills and resources.

Why do people become entrepreneurs?

Research suggests four motives:
- Dramatic change in personal situation (unemployment, divorce)
- Availability of resources (idea, money)
- Certain entrepreneurial skills
- Example of another successful entrepreneur.

Typical entrepreneurial traits

The entrepreneur is the key to the successful launch of any business. He / she is the person who perceives the market opportunity and then has the motivation, drive and ability to mobilise resources to meet it.

Although it is difficult to describe a typical entrepreneur, they share certain characteristics or traits:
- **Self-confident all-rounder:** The person who can make the product, market it and count the money
- **The ability to bounce back:** The person who can cope with making mistakes and still has the confidence to try again
- **Innovative skills:** Not necessarily an 'inventor' in the traditional sense but a person who is able to carve out a new niche in the marketplace, often invisible to others
- **Results-orientated:** To make the business successful requires a drive that only comes from setting goals and targets and getting pleasure from achieving them
- **Professional risk-taker:** To succeed means taking measured risks. Often the successful entrepreneur exhibits a step-by-step approach to risk-taking, at each stage exposing him / herself to only a limited, measured amount of personal risk and moving from one stage to another only as each decision is proved
- **Total commitment:** Hard work, energy and single-mindedness are essential elements in the entrepreneurial profile.

Entrepreneurs are risk-takers, willing to roll the dice with their money or their reputations on the line in support of an idea or enterprise. They willingly assume responsibility for the success or failure of a venture and are answerable for all its facets. The buck not only stops at their desk, it starts there too.
VICTOR KIAM

The "entrepreneurial state of mind" is an attitude that says, in short: "I didn't just come to play the game – I came to win".
GORDON BATY

Note that the entrepreneurial characteristics required to launch a business successfully are often not the same as those required for growth and, even more frequently, not the same as those required to manage the business once it grows to any size. The role of the entrepreneur needs to change with the business as it develops and grows. In particular, the management skills of the entrepreneur – in managing staff, managing his / her own time, and in strategic planning – become more important as the business grows.

Success factors

Research suggests that successful entrepreneurs share some common factors. Which of the success factors in the panel do you have?

SUCCESS & FAILURE FACTORS: WHICH DO YOU HAVE?

Ability to accept uncertainty (including financial uncertainty)
Ability to focus
Ability to sell
Clear initial goals
Common-sense
Creativity
Experience
Expertise
Flexibility
Good health
Guts
Hard work
Integrity
Leadership
Luck
Management skills
Motivation
Passion
Perseverance
Self-confidence
Social skills
Support of a network
Support of family
Willingness to be different

SELF-ASSESSMENT

Before you decide to start your own business, know that:

- The average working week of a self-employed person is 64 hours. In almost half of those businesses, the spouse / partner is also involved for another 21 hours (total, 85 hours)
- Most people do not increase their income by becoming self-employed
- One in five entrepreneurs do not earn anything in the first 18 months in business
- Support of the spouse / partner is a critical factor in the success or failure of a start-up business.

Running your own business demands a lot of commitment. It is both physically and mentally demanding. Therefore, it is very important to ask yourself why you want to become self-employed. This will take some soul-searching but it is vital to the decision to go ahead. If your motivation is not strong enough, you will not last the race.

You also need to be sure that you have your family's support.

Self-assessment

The questions in the **Self-assessment** panel on the next page will help you assess your own suitability for starting and running a business. Write down your answers. If you have business partners, they should answer these questions too.

Relationship with family

Your relationship with your family is going to change because of your new business.

You will no longer have a regular income – some months you may have no pay-check at all. Can your family survive on what your spouse / partner earns?

You will be working long hours, through weekends and at times when other people are off. Your working hours will be irregular – nothing to do for a while and then several urgent jobs all to be done at once. You will be under pressure, since you will no longer have a boss to take the final responsibility for everything – you will now be the boss.

You will have more at risk than just your money – your reputation, savings, borrowings, even your ego are also at risk.

All this will affect your relationship with your family. Are you ready?

Why not discuss the situations in the panel with your family? It will help you – and them – understand what lies ahead and how you will react to the choices that may need to be made.

OBJECTIVES

o Understand the need for commitment

o Understand the need for family support

o Be able to carry out a self-assessment

Beware of undertaking too much at the start. Be content with quite a little. Allow for accidents. Allow for human nature, especially your own.
ARNOLD BENNETT

Anyone who wants to achieve a dream must stay strong, focused and steady.
ESTEE LAUDER

I do not believe a man can ever leave his business. He ought to think of it by day and dream of it by night.
HENRY FORD

7

What positives do you bring to the business:

Network of useful contacts?	☐ YES ☐ NO
Support of your partner / spouse?	☐ YES ☐ NO
Support of your family and friends?	☐ YES ☐ NO
Finance?	☐ YES ☐ NO
Other? (list)	

What personal characteristics do you bring to the business:

Health?	Good / OK / Bad
Endurance?	Good / OK / Bad
Flexibility?	Good / OK / Bad
Creativity?	Good / OK / Bad
Honesty?	Good / OK / Bad
Confidence?	Good / OK / Bad
Ability to handle stress?	Good / OK / Bad
Other? (list)	
	Good / OK / Bad
	Good / OK / Bad
	Good / OK / Bad

What time commitments do you bring to the business:

Social activities	hrs / week
Family	hrs / week
Hobbies	hrs / week
Other (list)	
	hrs / week
	hrs / week
	hrs / week
Total time commitment outside the business	hrs / week
How much could you reduce these to make time for the business?	hrs / week

What financial commitments do you bring to the business?

Household expenses	€___/ week
Loan repayments	€___/ week
Savings / pension	€___/ week
Hobbies / holidays	€___/ week
Other (list)	
	€___/ week
	€___/ week
	€___/ week
Total financial commitments	€___/ week
How much could you reduce these to develop the business?	€___/ week

Think positive

Don't be alarmed by this section on self-assessment. It is merely pointing out the reality of self-employment. If you don't believe it, check with someone you know who has recently started their own business.

And above all – don't let this section put you off. There are positives to running your own business:

- You can organise your own working hours

- You can do the tasks you like to do and pay other people to do the things you dislike
- You are in control of your own destiny
- You learn a lot
- You deal with all kinds of different situations
- You deal with a lot of different people
- You get a great sense of achievement
- People respect and admire entrepreneurs.

SITUATIONS TO DISCUSS WITH YOUR FAMILY

- The kids need new shoes. The business needs a new piece of equipment that costs €100. There is only €100 in the bank. Which comes first?
- A big order comes in (Congratulations!). For the next two weeks, you need to work at least 14 hours every day (including weekends) to meet this order. It is also your turn to look after the kids this weekend. What are you going to do?
- You promised your spouse / partner a night out. That night a client insists on meeting you. Which comes first?
- You have booked a holiday and the whole family is really looking forward to it. Suddenly, the person who was supposed to look after the business while you are away cancels. You cannot find another replacement on such short notice. What happens?
- A deadline needs to be met. You get ill. Who will take over the running of the business while you are out sick?
- The business is not going as well as expected. Your business needs an extra loan to survive. Your partner / spouse wants you to quit. What happens?
- Your business has a cashflow problem. As a result, you have not been able to take out a salary for the past two months and some of your household bills (telephone, gas, electricity) are running behind. How long will that be acceptable to your partner / spouse?

Reproduced from LOOK BEFORE YOU LEAP *by permission of the Department of Enterprise, Trade & Employment and the Department of Social, Community & Family Affairs.*

CHANGES IN YOUR LIFE

Do you accept the changes the business is going to bring to your life:

Financial insecurity?	☐ YES ☐ NO
Long working hours?	☐ YES ☐ NO
Irregular working hours?	☐ YES ☐ NO
Pressure?	☐ YES ☐ NO
Risk?	☐ YES ☐ NO
Relationship with family?	☐ YES ☐ NO

DEVELOPING YOUR IDEA

Developing your idea to its fullest potential involves creative thinking. This section provides an overview of some of the most common creative thinking techniques. They will help you to identify new ideas, develop your existing idea and create new opportunities.

Thinking

We all think in two stages. The first stage is to look, simplify what we see, recognise and name what we see, then filter it through our experience and knowledge. In the second stage, we then judge and conclude. Unfortunately, we spend most of our time thinking in the second stage. With creative thinking, most of the time is spent in the first stage of thinking.

Look below. What do you see?

●

Your answer is probably: "A black dot".

Yes, there is a black dot, but there is also more text, white space, etc. By jumping straight into second stage thinking, you missed all the surroundings. You did not take time to sit back, relax and look a little bit longer. You rushed for the obvious answer. But, by taking time to step back, you will see more and, by seeing more, you will also see more possibilities. That is the idea behind creative thinking.

As an entrepreneur, it is important to spend time looking at your idea and trying to come up with new possibilities, extra features, alternatives, etc. This will not only give you an even better understanding of your idea, it will improve it and will make you more competitive. This kind of creative thinking should be an ongoing process to keep your business competitive.

Steps in creative thinking

Move away:
- Widen perception
- Question assumptions (Why not? What if?)
- Break the rules
- Make associations.

Bring yourself back into the real world:
- Evaluate
- Judge
- Tried before?
- Will it work?

One sound idea is all you need to achieve success.
NAPOLEON HILL

I work from details outward to the general and I don't stop developing big ideas until I have worked out the minutest detail.
RAY KROC, McDonalds

We haven't got the money, so we've got to think.
LORD RUTHERFORD

Attempt the impossible to improve your work.
BETTE DAVIS

Technique 1: Brainstorming

- Get a group together (minimum four people, preferably more)
- Define a problem and discuss it
- Redefine the problem
- Do a practice run to warm up the mind – for example: *How many uses can you find for a paperclip?*

In brainstorming:
- Aim to generate as many ideas as possible
- All ideas are acceptable
- The crazier the idea the better
- Select the craziest idea and brainstorm that idea for a while.

Technique 2: Attribute listing

This technique is best used when you are thinking of adapting or developing an existing product or service. Take the particular product and list its attributes: for example, shape, size, design, materials, colour, functions and cost. Then take each attribute and find as many alternatives to it as possible.

Technique 3: Who, what, where, when, why, how

Tease out different perspectives and ideas with any product, service, problem or situation, using the six prompts above.

Technique 4: Assumption-smashing

List the assumptions of the problem or idea, then explore what happens if you drop assumptions. For example, why assume that a particular product should be made of plastic. What if it were made of something else?

Technique 5: Discontinuity

Disrupt your own patterns:
- Programme interruptions in your day
- Do something you have never done before or read something you would not normally read
- Watch some different TV programmes.

Minimum viable product

Although it's good to spend time thinking about new possibilities and extra features for your product, in the early stages your challenge is likely to be more about producing an initial batch of product for sale. If yours is a (potentially) complex product, either to produce or for the customer to understand and use, consider launching with a 'minimum viable product'.

A MVP is the least complicated, least well-featured version of your product that will be acceptable to your potential customers.

It's not simply a cut-down version – if your product doesn't do the job it's meant, it won't simply sell – but a version that focuses on meeting customers' immediate needs, leaving other wants to be satisfied by later versions of the product.

A classic example of a MVP is often given in the area of personal transportation. While a bicycle is not a perfect substitute for a car, it offers people who might otherwise have to walk to work the opportunity to travel faster and go longer distances. A motorbike extends the speed and distance capability, until the customer is able to afford to buy a car.

What's your MVP?

Putting it into practice

Developing an idea is only part of the battle. The idea must also work in practice. Therefore, it is important to ask yourself some critical questions about your business and your product / service. Write your answers below. Copy this page before answering, so that you can use these pages to develop and test other ideas later

WHAT KIND OF BUSINESS ARE YOU THINKING ABOUT?

Are you starting to make?	☐ YES ☐ NO
Are you starting in retail?	☐ YES ☐ NO
Are you starting in import / export?	☐ YES ☐ NO
Are you starting a service?	☐ YES ☐ NO
Are you starting a brokerage?	☐ YES ☐ NO
Are you starting in leisure?	☐ YES ☐ NO
Are you starting online?	☐ YES ☐ NO
A combination of some of the above?	☐ YES ☐ NO

Describe your idea:

IDEA ASSESSMENT

Why is it a good idea?
On what assumptions is your opinion based?
How can you prove that those assumptions are correct?
What types of customer will be interested in your product / service? Why?
Who will be paying your invoice? What do *they* want?
List four reasons why the idea may not work:
List four reasons why your idea will work:
What is different about this idea from others already in the marketplace?
Why are those differences important?
What if you changed the product / service in some way?
Make a list of people you know who might be able to help you with the research or whose opinion you trust. Ask their opinion about your idea. Ask them to be critical and honest.

IDENTIFYING FUTURE TRENDS

If you want to be in business for a long time, you need to develop a vision of the future and the place of your business in that future. You need not only to be aware of the trends in your market area (technology, competition, trade regulations, etc.) but also have a sense of the general direction in which the world is developing. Questions to consider are: What will Ireland look like in 2030 – or even in 2050? Where will your business fit? What should you be doing to prepare?

Consider these current trends:

- To protect themselves from crime and hostility, people are retreating into the safe environment of the home
- People want to do exciting things but also want to be safe at the same time – emotional escape in a risk-free fantasy world. Consider changes in food (exotic meals), shopping (fun shopping), interactive movies and games, etc.
- Luxuries are no longer big purchases but include "rewards" like handmade chocolates, week-end breaks and expensive restaurant meals. Spending patterns are becoming less predictable
- Technology allows products to be focused on very specific needs
- People are less concerned about job security and more willing to change jobs several times during their careers to pursue new opportunities
- Consumers are more health-conscious and critical about the behaviour of companies and the quality of products and services
- People have higher expectations of life. They want to achieve more – often materially
- Time is a major factor in most people's lives. They feel a need to cram activities into the day (reading, movie, theatre, socialising, being a good parent or partner, do a course, make a career, etc.)
- Older people stay healthier much longer and age does not dictate the pace of life any more. Old people act young
- Society and business is more and more influenced by women.

Read science fiction or books by writers like William Gibson. Much of what was written as science fiction 20 or 30 years ago is now part of our everyday lives.

Train yourself to watch trends. Look for:

- Changes in food, new products, trendy restaurants
- The introduction of new products (failures and successes)

You have to look where the (hockey) puck is going to be, not where it is now.
WAYNE GRETSKY

13

- Changes in family structure
- Changes in demographics
- Changes in work environment
- Changes in environmental behaviour
- Whether there is optimism or pessimism in relation to the economy
- New cultures
- New words (Twitter, Watson, AI, screenager)
- Science fiction becoming real.

When you examine trends, be aware of the exponential nature of change today. Everything is doubling in speed, based on Moore's Law (that computers double in complexity every two years – and, at the same, halve in price). This now applies in many fields – for example, health, sensors, Artificial Intelligence, nano-technology, robotics, genetics, biology, physics, etc.

Then watch for the balancing impact of the Action = Reaction principle. For example:

Action
- Rapid change of technology, increasing role of computers
- Globalisation of markets due to easy access of information and technology
- Re-engineering, jobs replaced or supported by use of new technology
- Multi-cultural influences due to all information available

Reaction
- Back to nature in response to technology
- Back to old values / culture as those things are familiar to us
- Back into our homes to protect us from the outside (hostile) world
- Filters on information (for example, the Internet Nanny)
- Simplifying information
- Escapism in movies, computer games, adventure trips, etc.
- To balance the stress, 'perks' to cheer us (massage, fancy dinners, clothes, etc.).

Some other things to think about:
- The use of drugs for specific purposes (memory enhancers, warfare)
- Development of genetic engineering
- The role of computers and telecommunications in our society
- Nano-technology (machines the size of an atom).

What are your predictions for Ireland in 2030 and 2050? Write them down. Where does your business fit within these?

MARKET RESEARCH

Marketing is about keeping your customers central in your thinking, behaviour and planning. To do that, you need a combination of information, vision and creativity. One of the techniques to get information is market research, which has three functions:

- **Informing:** Consumer behaviour, market trends, developments abroad
- **Evaluating:** Are goals achieved?
- **Experimenting:** Testing markets or products.

Why do market research?

Market research is the core of your business and business plan. It is important that you:

- Are aware of market developments
- Find out for yourself whether you can approach people at all kinds of levels
- Find out whether you can sell (if not, you will have to find someone to do it for you)
- Find out whether there is a market for your product / service, how big it is, how it can be reached, etc.
- Are well-prepared before you commit funds (your own or other people's) to your business
- Are able to show potential financiers that you have taken the trouble to gather the necessary information
- Are able to show that you know your stuff.

But the overwhelming reason for doing market research is to prove the commercial viability of your project – to yourself!

Making your market research practical

Market research is often considered by entrepreneurs to be too theoretical to be bothered with. That's dangerous and wrong:

- Dangerous because without market research you may start a business or develop a product / service for which there is no demand
- Wrong because market research can be very practical.

Practical market research includes things as simple as:

- Counting the cars on your competitors' parking lot (to tell you how many customers they get and how well-off they are)
- Counting the people passing by the premises you are planning to rent (big stores like Marks & Spencer sometimes do this for months before deciding on a location for a new shop)

OBJECTIVES

- o Understand market research techniques
- o Apply these techniques to your own product / service

Market research is about listening to people, analysing the information to help organisations make better decisions and **reducing the risk**. It is about analysing and interpreting data to build information and knowledge that can be used to predict future, actions or behaviours.
ESOMAR

- Counting the waste bags outside the backdoor of a restaurant (to give you some idea of the volume of their business)
- Counting visitors to a competitor's website
- Checking competitors' presence on social media channels
- Checking the number of trucks delivering supplies to competitors (on the basis that level of their purchases gives you an insight into their sales)
- Counting the numbers of customers walking into a competitors' office or shop
- Knocking on every door in an area in which you are planning to open an outlet (to ask whether there is a demand, at what price, etc.)
- Collecting all your competitors' brochures and price lists (to find out what they are offering and at what prices)
- Checking where your competitors advertise and how big an advertisement they take.

Note that market research should be an ongoing process. It should not stop after the business has started (or the product / service has been launched) but should become an integral part of your business.

Understand buying criteria

A potential customer who calls a plumber in the middle of the night is far less interested in the price of the plumber's services than in their (immediate) availability. In contrast, if the same customer is looking to update the company's website, quality (as evidenced by reputation – in social media perhaps?) trumps availability, as there are likely to be many potentially suitable suppliers.

Whoever your customer and whatever their buying criteria, you need to understand them if you are to address them in your value proposition and in your marketing.

Sources of information

When you are looking for information as part of your desk research, there is an almost endless list of sources of information, including:
- Your local public library
- Central Statistics Office (**www.cso.ie**)
- Enterprise Ireland (**www.enterprise-ireland.com**)
- Government Departments and State agencies (**www.irlgov.ie / www.basis.ie**)
- Business magazines and newspapers
- Banks and credit unions

- Business Innovation Centres
- Local Enterprise Offices (**www.localenterprise.ie**)
- Area Partnership Companies
- LEADER companies
- Professional associations / trade bodies
- Telephone directories
- Trade exhibitions and conferences
- Competitors' catalogues, brochures and price lists
- Professional advisers (accountants, solicitors, consultants)
- Friends, especially those already in business
- Chambers of Commerce (**www.chambers.ie**)
- Customers (existing or potential)
- Local authorities
- Internet.

And don't overlook social media as a source of information – often it will be the most accessible and richest source you use.

Many of these sources – especially social media – will give you information free of charge, or at very little cost. Recognise their help where you can – you'll be amazed at how much even just a "Thank You" will be appreciated – and how much you will benefit if you go back for more information.

Remember:

- Seek information from a variety of sources, not just 'experts'
- Get feedback from a variety of sources
- Let people play 'devil's advocate' and argue against you
- Ask 'stupid' questions – you may get some very clever answers
- Look for yourself – don't assume anything.

Doing your own market research

Structure your market research to make sure you collect all the information you need. The structure depends on your product / service, your budget and the time available but ought to cover:

- **Problem definition:** What do you want to find out?
- **Desk research:** Consulting directories, magazines and newspapers and the Internet
- **Pre-study field research:** A first test to see whether you are on the right track
- **Concept questionnaire:** Your initial questions
- **Testing the questionnaire:** Make sure that the questions can be understood and will give you useful answers
- **Field research:** Asking the questions
- **Data processing:** Processing the results
- **Reporting:** The final stage.

Research techniques

There are many ways of researching your idea, including:

- **Qualitative / quantitative:** Quantitative involves researching figures and percentages; qualitative means researching opinions, reasons why, etc.
- **Consumer / distribution / industrial:** You can research the end user of your product, how the product is brought to the end user, or how the product is made
- **Questionnaires / observation:** You can ask people personally, by mail, by phone, or observe their behaviour (which may be different from what they tell you)
- **Ad hoc / panel:** You can do once-off research, or research a panel for a longer period of time
- **Group / single:** You can interview a group of people or every person in your sample individually
- **Open / half-open / closed questions:** You can ask open questions (no control over the answer), half-open questions (give different options), or closed questions (yes or no).

MARKET RESEARCH: A CASE STUDY

A Japanese company had plans to build a paper factory in Georgia, USA. They thought it would be useful to know the production capacity of the local competitors. But these figures were not readily available. So the company started counting the number of train wagons leaving the factories. This gave them the volume of production. Although the wagons were closed, the residue left on the rails after the train had passed told them what the train was carrying. Volume multiplied by content gave them the production capacity of the competitors' plant.

The starting point is to define the problem: What do you want to know? Write it down below.

MARKET RESEARCH

I expect my market research to tell me:

When you start your desk research, collect information from as many sources as possible. List below the sources of information you intend to use.

POTENTIAL SOURCES OF INFORMATION

1.
2.
3.

After you have completed your desk research (and only then), start designing a questionnaire for the target customer groups you have identified. This will need some research in the target groups itself (location, availability, language, level of questioning, perceptions, etc.).

Go back to basics. Ask yourself: Who? What? Why? When? Where? Make a list of questions you want to ask below.

QUESTIONNAIRE DESIGN: QUESTIONS YOU WANT TO ASK

Select only the most relevant questions. Depending on the approach you plan to take, you may need to take the length of the questionnaire into consideration. If it is too long, people won't want to answer it – especially in the case of direct mail or questioning over the phone. Then test your questionnaire with a small group of people to make sure that it is clear and user-friendly. If you get a poor response here, redesign your questionnaire and test it again.

When the questionnaire is complete, you are ready to do the field research. If your aim is to get quantitative information, the number of people questioned should be sufficient to be statistically valid (minimum between 500 and 1,000). Note that it's quite usual to get a very low response rate to questionnaires.

Reporting results

It is useful to summarise the results of your desk and field research.

Overall, the more time spent on this market research phase before you start your business, the more it will benefit you by laying the basis for your business plan.

MARKET RESEARCH CHECKLIST

Does your market research cover:

Market size?	☐ YES ☐ NO
Market structure?	☐ YES ☐ NO
Market trends?	☐ YES ☐ NO
Market potential?	☐ YES ☐ NO
Market share?	☐ YES ☐ NO
Competitor activity?	☐ YES ☐ NO
Competitor prices?	☐ YES ☐ NO
Competitor products / services?	☐ YES ☐ NO
User attitudes / behaviour?	☐ YES ☐ NO
Government factors?	☐ YES ☐ NO
Economic factors?	☐ YES ☐ NO
Demographic factors?	☐ YES ☐ NO

The real question that you are looking for the answer to is:

Is this idea worth pursuing further?	☐ YES ☐ NO

BUSINESS MODEL CANVAS

o Understand the Business Model Canvas

o Be able to use the Business Model Canvas

Based on Alex's PhD thesis (*The Business Model Ontology – A Proposition in a Design Science Approach*) at the University of Lausanne, Switzerland in 2004, in 2010 Alex Osterwalder and Yves Pigner wrote a classic book, *Business Model Generation*, in which they launched the Business Model Canvas.

The Business Model Canvas is a one-page format for developing new business models or for documenting existing models. It consists of nine panels:

- The first three – Key Activities, Key Resources and Key Partners – describe the infrastructure of the business model
- The offering is covered in the Value Proposition panel
- Customers are covered in three more panels – Customer Segments. Customer Relationships and Channels
- Finances are captured in the Cost Structure and Revenue Streams panels.

Each panel offers a number of questions to kickstart your thinking. By documenting everything you know (or need to know) about these key elements in the panels, the connections between them, you capture your business model on a single page – much easier than asking someone to read a 40-page business plan or offering them a coffee-stained napkin from your first planning session!

The beauty of the Business Model Canvas lies in its simplicity and ease of communication. But as designers know only too well, simplicity is never easy. Often, the Business Model Canvas is at its most powerful at the very earliest stages of your business / business model development, when it allows you to see clearly how the different elements interact or when your thinking has crystallised and your business model is clear – in the middle stages, it's easy to get overwhelmed in detail.

The Business Model Canvas

TESTING YOUR IDEA

Ultimately, the best way to test your idea is to sell it in the marketplace. If it's sells, it's a good idea – if not, then it's not a good idea. Simple, direct, unequivocal.

But for most start-ups, the (relatively) high costs of getting a first product to market, coupled with the low likelihood of success (90% fail), and the consequences – financial and personal – of failure, mean that this is a far too high-risk strategy. They need some way of finding out in advance whether their product will sell – and how to improve the odds in their favour.

The answer is testing.

Even at this very early stage, you need to test your product in two ways:

- Market need / acceptance
- Financially.

Testing for market need is a key part of your market research. It means understanding your customers, their problems and the cause(s) of those problems – and ensuring that your product (even if it's only a MVP) is a real solution to their problems (or at least some of them). For example, for a variety of reasons and excuses, most people manage their personal finances poorly, despite the wide range of personal finance books, tools and training available. It's rarely a matter of lack of intelligence; perhaps it's lack of discipline to stick to a system; but perhaps it's because most personal finance sellers and advisers use jargon that their customers don't understand. Simple language with clear explanations might sell more financial products than any sophisticated capability.

Testing financially means checking first that likely sales revenues will cover costs – if not, initially, then within a reasonable timeframe – and that those sales revenues are achievable. A quick way to test the latter is to divide annual sales units by the number of working days, and then by the number of working hours in each day, to get the number of units to be sold on average in an hour. Is this achievable – every hour of every working day?

At its heart, testing your idea means developing a series of assumptions – for example, if your idea is to offer ready-to-cook-at-home meals for sale to commuters on their way home, your assumptions may include:

- People don't have time to prepare their main daily meal from scratch each day but don't want to eat out every day either
- They want do want to engage in some preparation – not just stick a package in the microwave

- Understand the need to test your idea
- Understand how to test your idea

21

- They want healthy food
- They associate healthy food with buying on the day of eating – but don't have time to shop for food each day
- They will pay a premium – though not a huge premium – for a product that meets these needs.

Talking to potential customers – at commuter train and bus stations on their way home perhaps – is the first step in testing your idea. The point is not to get exact results but, through quick estimates, to reduce risk – if necessary, by taking the ultimate step of not proceeding with the idea!

TRAINING FOR ENTREPRENEURS

Potential entrepreneurs need (or may need, depending on their circumstances) three kinds of training:

- In the specific stages / techniques of starting up a business
- In specific skills useful for a start-up, which they lack from previous experience
- In specific skills useful once the business is up and running, which they lack from previous experience.

Few people have the first, since training for start-ups is not on many school or college curricula. This guide, and many of the books and websites available, attempt to fill the gap. There are also Start Your Own Business courses available from a variety of sources, including the Local Enterprise Offices, to meet this need.

Training Needs Analysis

Training in other skills, whether pre- or post-start-up, requires a Training Needs Analysis. This simply means that you list your present skills, compare them against the skills you believe that you need and plan to do something about the difference.

Answer the questions in the panel to prepare your own Training Needs Analysis. If you have business partners, they should complete this analysis also.

TRAINING NEEDS ANALYSIS

List your skills:

List your practical experience:

What skills do you think you need to **start** your business?

What skills do you think you need to **run** your business, once it has been started?

What skills are you missing?

Sources of training

There are many organisations that provide training in specific subject areas – however, only a few provide a general training in entrepreneurship or how to start a business.

Before signing up for a course, talk to people who have already taken the course or programme you are considering and get their opinions.

Remember also that you cannot know everything. Whatever your own background, you will have to buy in some expertise – from accountants, solicitors, computer experts or consultants. But to give yourself a general understanding of a range of topics, even if the detailed work is done by someone else, attend courses outside your own immediate area of interest.

TRAINING CHECKLIST

Before you commit to a course or programme, check:

- **Time necessary *versus* time available:** There is no point starting a course if you don't have the time to do it – and remember, there'll probably be some work to be done outside class too

- **Entry level:** Have you got the necessary educational background / practical experience to benefit from the course?

- **Background of participants:** Who are the other people on the course? Will their needs be different from yours (and prevent you from achieving your training objectives)?

- **Course coverage:** What does it cover? Is this relevant to you?

- **Cost:** How much does the course cost? Are there grants available? Do you qualify for a grant?

- **Available back-up support:** What happens if you have problems during the course? Afterwards?

- **Accreditation:** Is the course officially recognised? Do you get a certificate on completion?

Apart from the usual sources of training above, try talking to other entrepreneurs – not just locally, but also in other countries across the world through start-up forums or conferences. Consider doing an entrepreneurship apprenticeship.

And remember that one of the fundamental skills of an entrepreneur is selling. If you already can sell (congratulations, you're in a minority!), go on a sales course to improve your skills – everyone else, go on a course to learn how to sell.

START-UP ALTERNATIVES

If you want to run your own business, there are alternatives to starting it yourself. The main choices are:

- To spin-out a business from your current employment
- To buy an existing business
- To buy into a franchise
- To get involved in network marketing
- To join an existing start-up.

Spin-outs

A 'spin-out' (or sometimes 'spin-off') is a business created from within an existing business. An employee with a business idea is supported initially to develop the idea by their employer. When they are ready to leave employment to take the idea further, often their employer takes an equity stake in the business and may provide access to specialised equipment or resources on an ongoing basis. Often spin-outs occur among scientific research teams where the market potential of the research discovery does not fit with the employer's strategic direction.

Buying an existing business

Buying an existing business is a sensible alternative to starting a business from scratch. The main advantage is that you acquire a business with existing products, markets, customers, staff, etc. and do not have to build it all up yourself. The disadvantage is that you have to commit a considerable up-front investment to acquire the business and may have to add to this to develop the business further. You also need to know why the business is being sold – perhaps it is in trouble.

Buying an existing business needs a methodical approach. Insist on both historical figures (preferably three years or more) and future projections. Have the information checked by a person you trust or hire an expert. Do your own Strengths / Weaknesses / Opportunities / Threats (SWOT) analysis, get feedback from clients, suppliers and competitors. Particular areas to look into are:

- Financial data
- Management and key personnel
- Recent investments (or lack of)
- Product development / improvements (or lack of)
- Innovation (or lack of)
- Use of modern technology (or lack of)
- Hidden liabilities.

OBJECTIVES

o   Be aware of the alternatives to a start-up

o   Understand the risks of buying an existing business

o   Understand how to evaluate an existing business for sale

o   Understand the franchise concept and its advantages and disadvantages

o   Understand how to evaluate a potential franchise

o   Understand the network marketing concept

o   Understand how to evaluate a potential network marketing business

Never acquire a business you don't know how to run.
ROBERT W JOHNSON

25

You need to know how much more money you will have to put into the business, on top of the purchase price, and how risky is this investment. How long will it take to recover your investment?

When you think you are ready to buy a specific business, take out a sheet of paper and write down your answers to the questions in the checklist. Only buy when you are sure that the business is right for you. Above all, make sure that you take professional advice before committing to buying. Remember, buying the business is only the beginning. You still need to work through the rest of this guide to develop a business plan for your 'new' business – while you run it on a day-to-day basis.

BUYING A BUSINESS

Why is the business for sale?
What is the business of the company?
How is it organised?
What is its position in the marketplace?
What are its future prospects?
Is there a current business plan?
What does it tell me?
Does the culture of the company fit my style of working and managing?
How dependent is the company on the current owner / managers?

Buying into a franchise

Across the world, there are over thousands of franchised businesses – the International Franchise Association lists 1,400 – covering almost every industry. Some are international brands like McDonald's; others are national brands like The Wine Buff; a few are much smaller, local opportunities.

When you buy a franchise, you are buying the right to use a specific trademark or business concept, which has been tested in practice. The chief benefit is that you are able to capitalise on the business format, trade name, and support system provided by the franchisor.

You pay an initial upfront fee for the rights to open your franchise. This fee may include things like training costs, start-up promotional costs, stock, equipment / fixtures (you may be required to purchase or lease specific equipment and fixtures from the franchisor), and any other costs that are necessary to start your business. Usually, the franchisor helps you during start-up, with selection of premises and equipment, a business plan, raising finance, and publicity. In return, the franchisor supplies a detailed operational manual, which sets out exactly how you should run the franchise.

You also have to pay ongoing fees to maintain the rights to your franchise. Most franchisors charge a royalty fee – typically a percentage of your gross sales, ranging from 1% to as much as 15%. It is also usual for franchisees to pay into a co-operative national advertising and promotional fund that benefits all franchises through increased exposure to the common trade name.

The advantages of buying a franchise are:

- Franchises traditionally have a much lower failure rate than other start-up businesses, since most of the problems have already been discovered and solved

- You get a complete package, including trademarks, easy access to an established product, proven marketing method, equipment, stock, etc.

- You have the buying power of the entire network, which can help you against larger competitors

- Many franchisors provide financial and accounting systems, on-going training and support, research and development, sales and marketing assistance, planning and forecasting, stock management, etc.

- Some franchisors help with site selection, making sure that your business is located in an area where it can thrive

- You benefit from national or regional advertising and promotional campaigns by the franchisor.

But, as in anything, there are disadvantages, too. These can include:

- The essence of a franchise – buying and operating a proven concept – can make it seem like you're more of a manager than a boss

- It can take a good deal of cash to open and operate a franchise. Upfront costs can be significant, and ongoing royalty fees may impact on your cashflow

- Just as a franchisor's reputation can benefit you, the franchisor's problems are also your problems

- Your franchise agreement is a binding contract, and can be quite restrictive.

Although you own the business, its operation is governed by the terms of the franchise agreement. Therefore, you should have your lawyer and / or accountant review the franchise agreement before signing anything.

Before you decide on a franchise, talk to other franchisees. Ask about their experiences. Would they do it again? What would they do differently? Listen carefully to their answers.

BUYING INTO A FRANCHISE CHECKLIST

Does the franchisor have a track record of success?

☐ YES ☐ NO

What will it cost me?
☐ Once current income?
☐ Twice current income?
☐ More?

How much can I expect to make?
☐ Once current income?
☐ Twice current income?
☐ More?

Will the franchisor give me an exclusive territory for the period of the franchise? ☐ YES ☐ NO

Will the franchisor assist me with:

- A management training programme? ☐ YES ☐ NO
- An employee training programme? ☐ YES ☐ NO
- A PR and advertising programme? ☐ YES ☐ NO
- Raising capital? ☐ YES ☐ NO
- Borrowing money? ☐ YES ☐ NO
- Merchandising ideas? ☐ YES ☐ NO
- Finding a suitable location? ☐ YES ☐ NO

How long has the franchisor been operating?
☐ Less than 3 years?
☐ More than 3 years?

Has the franchisor a reputation for fair dealing with its franchisees? ☐ YES ☐ NO

Has the franchisor enough finance itself to carry out its plans?

☐ YES ☐ NO

What happens when I want to leave / give up? Can I sell the business to anyone I like? ☐ YES ☐ NO

Has the franchiser shown me any certified figures indicating exact net profits of one or more franchisees, which I have personally checked with them? ☐ YES ☐ NO

Has the franchisor investigated me carefully enough to be sure that I can successfully operate at a profit to both of us?

☐ YES ☐ NO

Is my lawyer completely happy with the franchise contract?

☐ YES ☐ NO

Adapted from *Making Money* magazine by permission

Network marketing

As with franchising, everyone is familiar with network marketing, even though they may not know it by that name – it's often called multi-level marketing (MLM). Examples include:

- **Tupperware:** Household storage items
- **Herbalife:** Personal care and nutrition products
- **Amway:** Household products.

Network marketing skips the wholesalers and retailers in the distribution chain and delivers a product directly from the producer to the customer. This means quick delivery, good service and that the product is sold by people who know the product since they use it themselves.

Because there are no intermediaries between producer and customer, a large margin is available to pay people in the distribution chain. Distributors earn this margin by selling direct to customers and also from a royalty on sales made by other distributors whom they have introduced. The process is based on the idea that more gets sold by a lot of people each selling a little than by a small number of highly-effective salespeople on their own. Because all distributors are self-employed and self-motivated, only the successful survive. In the network, back-up is available to provide the members of the network with training, workshops, information materials, manuals, etc.

Unfairly, network marketing has a poor reputation – in part caused by its similarity in a number of respects to the now universally outlawed 'pyramid selling'. Network marketing, according to one researcher, is not a 'get rich quick' scheme – he says it is a 'get rich scheme for those prepared to perform consistent, persistent, productive, income-producing activities'. Even though it can be done part-time while you work at another job or in the home (and this is one of its key attractions), network marketing needs a lot of time and commitment not only in selling but also in learning about the products, in training in how to do the presentations, in developing and maintaining a network, delivering the products, book-keeping and administration, etc.

Therefore, it's just as important to write a business plan (see the next chapter, **STEADY**) for a network marketing business as for any other business idea.

Other alternatives

Other alternatives to the traditional start-up include:
- **Inheriting a business from a relative:** Nice, but you still have to run it afterwards, so you still need a business plan
- **Management or employee buy-outs:** Where a group of employees buys the business they work in from the owners – again, you will need a business plan to raise the necessary finance and to run the business after acquisition.

In every case, there is a need for planning. However you arrive at your chosen business, if it is to be successful, you need to work through this workbook and develop your business plan. That's what the next chapter is all about.

NETWORK MARKETING CHECKLIST

Can I do it part-time?	☐ YES ☐ NO
How good are the products?	☐ Very good? ☐ Good? ☐ OK?
What customer guarantees does the company give?	
	☐ No quibble?
	☐ Money back?
	☐ None?
What is the company's track record, history, management, financial standing, etc.?	☐ Very good? ☐ Good? ☐ OK?
What investment must I make at the start? €	
How much do I have to sell to break-even? €	
How much time do I need to invest?	
Am I prepared to recruit people I know for the network?	
	☐ YES ☐ NO
Have I met and discussed the scheme with existing distributors?	
	☐ YES ☐ NO
Do I believe the income figures they quote?	
	☐ YES ☐ NO

Join an existing start-up

You can also join an existing start up and step into a team and their idea. Make sure you understand the dynamics of the team, the shared vision and passion and where you can deliver value. Clarity is key, particularly around finance. Consider:

- How will you get paid?
- What risk(s) are you taking?
- What is your role going to be?).

Do your research and check out both the business idea and the people. All steps in the **READY** section apply.

STEADY

KEY QUESTIONS

Have you developed a strategy for your business?	☐ YES ☐ NO
Have you developed a customer profile?	☐ YES ☐ NO
Do you know how your business stands in the marketplace?	☐ YES ☐ NO
Have you developed a promotion strategy?	☐ YES ☐ NO
Have you identified the taxes for which you must register?	☐ YES ☐ NO
Have you decided how to organise your accounting?	☐ YES ☐ NO
Have you decided on a legal structure for your business?	☐ YES ☐ NO
Do you know how much money you need to start your business?	☐ YES ☐ NO
Have you identified sources of finance to meet this need?	☐ YES ☐ NO
Do you know your break-even point?	☐ YES ☐ NO
Have you prepared an operating budget?	☐ YES ☐ NO
Have you prepared cashflow projections?	☐ YES ☐ NO
Have you prepared a business plan?	☐ YES ☐ NO

These Key Questions are designed to focus your thoughts as you read this chapter. Think through your answers before you start to read the chapter. Then come back and write down your answers before moving on to the next chapter.

INTRODUCTION

o Understand the steps in a business start-up

o Understand the importance of business planning

o Develop a business plan

Success, as I see it, is a result not a goal.
GUSTAVE FLAUBERT

If we have a formula for growth, it has been:
Start with the best;
Learn from the best;
Expand slowly and solidify our position;
Then horizontally diversify our experience.
MARK McCORMACK, International Management Group

The only place success comes before work is in a dictionary.
ANON

The business plan is the most misunderstood element of starting a business. Too many people believe it needs only to be prepared when you are looking to raise finance. That's not true. Certainly, it is nearly impossible to raise finance without a business plan but the real value of a business plan comes in the thinking about your business that is necessary before you can write down what you plan to do. The business plan is the core of this chapter – and of starting a business.

Chapter structure

This is the longest and most detailed chapter in this guide, taking you through all the steps involved in starting your own business:

- Developing a strategy
- Innovation
- Competitiveness
- Marketing
- Products and production
- Staff
- Which legal structure?
- Business names
- Bank accounts
- Taxation
- Accounting
- Insurance
- Trading laws
- Premises
- Finance
- Financial projections
- Cashflow planning
- Sources of assistance
- Reducing risk
- Mentors
- Your business plan
- Pitching your plan
- Smell the flowers.

Your strategy sets the direction for your new business. Putting the strategy into action involves a wide range of topics including marketing, staff, financing, budgeting and cashflow, which are covered in the following sections. Sources of assistance – grants, advice, training, etc. – are covered next. Finally, this chapter takes you through the business planning process and helps you to complete a business plan that will help you manage your business as well as raise finance.

Everything you have learnt in this chapter is drawn together in your business plan. This is the real aim of the chapter – to help you to work your way through the thinking you need to do to develop a clear business plan. The thinking is the main thing; writing your business plan is the last 10%. But, unless you go that last 10%, you haven't finished the job.

Some other topics, such as quality, environmental and health and safety issues, are more appropriate to the on-going business and are covered in the next chapter, **GO!**.

DEVELOPING A STRATEGY

Developing a strategy for your business is as simple (or as complicated) as answering these questions:

- Where are we now?
- Where do we want to go?
- How and when will we get there?

Before deciding on your business' direction and course, you need to analyse the information already available to you and to collect more (see *Market Research* in **READY**). Do a SWOT analysis on the results of your market research, identifying each result as a:

- Strength
- Weakness
- Opportunity
- Threat.

Write your analysis in the panel.

OBJECTIVES

- o Understand strategy
- o Develop a strategy for your business

MARKET RESEARCH RESULTS

S	O
W	T

Next, re-read the section *Identifying Future Trends* in **READY**. Start developing a vision of the future and a place for your business in that future.

To begin to develop a strategy, consider:

- **Focus:** On what?
- **Growth, decline, stabilisation:** How is your market developing?
- **Maintain existing markets:** Will this be enough?
- **Life cycle of the product:** What stage are you at?
- **New markets:** Where? At what cost?
- **New products / services:** How?
- **National or international:** What are your ambitions?
- **Broad market or niche market:** Where are you aiming?
- **Innovation:** What part will it play?
- **Small or big steps:** Which are you most comfortable with?
- **Mission statement:** What is the mission statement for your business? How does this determine your strategy?

Long range planning does not deal with future decisions, but with the future of present decisions.
PETER F DRUCKER, Management author

Ultimately, vision gets translated into sales and profit, growth and return on investment, but the numbers come after the vision. In the old-style companies, the numbers are the vision.
JOHN NAISBITT, Futurist

33

Ask yourself the questions below. Write down your answers.

By answering the questions above, you have actually developed your strategy. You have set yourself targets and found ways of achieving them. You have probably found that you could be very specific about the first-year targets, but that 5-year and 10-year targets are more aspirational. But don't be misled by the simplicity of this approach to strategic planning. It looks simple. Maybe you found it simple to do. But it is critical to your business.

Every year, you should set yourself targets for the next year, keeping in mind your 10-year plan, which sets out the direction of your business. Compare it to a road map. The 10-year plan is the destination; the 1-year plans are the turns (right, left, straight, short cut, scenic route, stop-over, break for coffee, etc.). The direction you have decided needs to be checked on a regular basis to see whether your plans need adjustment.

The Strategic Box

Another way to developing a strategy for your business is to use the simple model below – the Strategic Box.

The thinking behind the Strategic Box is:
- Strategy is not linear
- The business environment is now too volatile and complex to be able to plan long-term.

The key factors therefore are constant movement – like riding a bicycle, if you stop moving, you fall off! – and the definition of the lens or filter, which helps you to simplify your environment.

You define six factors to create your Strategic Box, by writing a statement of what they mean for your business. The factors are:

- Values
- Passion
- Vision
- Mission
- Positioning
- Resourcing.

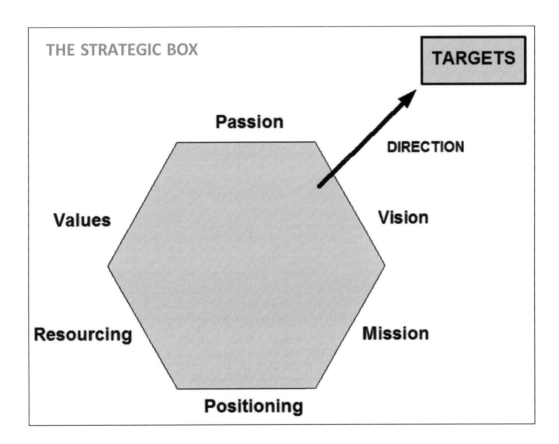

THE STRATEGIC BOX

Values are deeply personal. Unlike big businesses, which impose a set of corporate values on their staff in order to achieve uniformity, a start-up begins with the values of its founder – their own personal values. What the founder stands for – and what they won't stand for, too!

Values are about things like integrity and honesty in business, customer service, how you treat staff, and so on. Hard to write down – often only seen clearly when you are faced with difficult choices – but very important.

Passion is what separates successful businesses from the also-rans. Start-ups usually come into being because of the passion of the founder – to do something different, to go beyond existing boundaries, or to make customers' lives easier or better in some way.

Passion is what fuels your determination to succeed – it's what keeps you going through countless refinements of your product or service, until it is just right – like James Dyson, who only got his bag-less cyclone-powered vacuum-cleaner to work on his 5,127th attempt! That's passion at work!

Vision tells you where you are going, where you want to be. It answers the question: "Where do I want to go?".

What is your vision? What do you see in the future? Perhaps not days of wine and roses – but, seriously, what do you expect from your start-up? Why are you doing this? Your Vision must link into your values and your passion – there's no point setting out to achieve something that's either not you or that you won't like.

Setting out your vision for your start-up business helps you to identify the challenges that you will face in achieving it. Don't make the mistake of setting your aim too low – always aim higher than you expect to achieve, you may surprise yourself!

Mission statements set out in simple words what you (and your new business) are about and why it's important. If vision tells you where you want to be, a mission is what brings people along with you.

Positioning then tells you where other people – your customers and potential customers – think you are. You need to position your start-up in your potential customers' eyes as being suitable and sensible to do business with. That means creating the right image for your business from the beginning.

Resourcing is critical for start-ups, since they have very limited resources – it's their weakest link. But it's an important part of your strategy – knowing what resources you have, what you need and what to do about the difference.

Anything that is inside the "box" created by these statements is relevant; everything outside you ignore.

Then you add a seventh factor – **Targets** (weekly, monthly, annual) – to give you a sense of direction. Targets make clear your Vision and provide milestones on the way to achieving it. They provide an early warning system to tell you when you are wandering off-course or falling behind – and they provide encouragement as you tick them off ahead of schedule.

So strategy is not that difficult after all. Just seven factors.

Finally, you need to revisit your Strategic Box regularly. (Note that the Strategic Box concept works for both business and personal planning.)

INNOVATION

Innovation is one of the key success factors in any modern business.

The importance of innovation in the future is going to be even more significant due to constant change in technology, globalisation and the increased availability of information from, and convergence of, the Internet, TV, computer and telephone – not to mention alternative energies, bio-tech and nano-technology. To keep up with increasing competition, it is essential to be aware of those changes and constantly adjust the business to take account of new developments.

The management guru, Peter Drucker, defined innovation as "the purposeful and systematic search for change and opportunity". Thus, the techniques described in *Developing Your Idea* in **READY** are just as applicable in the management of innovation, to provide structure and continuity.

To manage innovation, it is important to create a constant flow of information through the business. To do this, you need to set up an innovation information system. This will bring together feedback from within your own business (for example, comments from your staff, clients and suppliers – all of which links with quality management) and combines it with outside sources such as competitors, newspapers, trade magazines, etc. To prevent any restriction of vision, the information sources should be widespread and some should be unrelated to business – to help you keep an open mind. Answering the following questions below will help you to develop your information system. Then go to the next section, *Competitiveness* and complete the *Information System Checklist* for your business.

INNOVATION

Internal
- How are you going to organise a system of feedback from your staff, clients and suppliers?
- What information / comments should you be looking for?

External
- What information sources are you going to access to keep informed?

Innovation should be part of the strategic plan (call it your 'innovation plan' to get the message across), as well as being part of your on-going product development.

Within innovation, there are three main directions:
- **Adjustment:** These are small changes that do not alter the function of your product or service

---

Business has only two functions: marketing and innovation.
PETER F DRUCKER, Management author

You see how things are, and you ask "Why?" But I dream of things that do not yet exist, and I ask "Why not?"
GEORGE BERNARD SHAW

Anything that won't sell, I don't want to invent.
THOMAS EDISON, Inventor

The glory went to the man who discovered electricity but it was the man who invented the electricity meter who made the money.
ANON

- **Modification:** Maintaining the technology used but changing the function (from clock to watch)
- **Renovation:** Same function, different technology (from vinyl records to CDs).

You must decide which of these directions (or what combination) is right for your business.

Organising innovation

Innovation does not happen; it must be planned for, organised and managed, through:

- Constant feedback and direct contact with customers
- Monthly review of information
- Regular brainstorm sessions with a group of people from different backgrounds
- A budget for innovation
- Appointing someone or making time yourself to search for new ideas (3M allows R&D workers to spend 15% of their time on their own ideas and aims to have 30% of turnover come from products developed in the last five years)
- Creating an 'idea box' (like a suggestions box) with cash prizes if ideas are used by the business
- Creating project teams (made up of both technicians and sales people) to work with clients on particular ideas and giving the team the power and authority to implement changes
- Creating a positive atmosphere in your business towards change.

Innovation does not always have to be a 'giant leap forward'. It can be a small step or, better still, a series of small steps (the 'continuous improvement' that is so much a part of quality management systems).

Always be on the look-out for ways to improve your product or service:

- Watch customers using your product for a while
- Swap jobs: Let technicians do the selling and let the sales team manage production
- Arrange service contracts with your customers to get constant feedback
- Let clients set the quality criteria.

You will always face resistance when you try to innovate. Don't let it get you down.

Without innovation, your business will stagnate and die. Don't let excuses for not innovating be heard in your business.

I would think of another fundamental need people have, and I would answer that need by offering a cheaper and more efficient service than anybody else could. In five years, I'd be a millionaire all over again.
HENRY FORD, Ford Motor Company

Sometimes when you innovate, you make mistakes. It is best to admit them quickly, and get on with improving your other innovations.
STEVE JOBS, Apple

COMPETITIVENESS

Being competitive is very simple: Be better than your competitors. This gives rise to two questions.

The first is how to define 'better'. This depends on what is important in the market in which the business is operating. In your market, does 'better' mean:

- Quicker?
- Friendlier?
- Cheaper?
- Higher quality?
- Technical back-up / after-sales service?
- A wide choice?
- Advice pre-purchase?

Does it mean all of these? Some of these? Something else entirely? You need to know, if you are to be able to achieve it.

Being competitive is closely connected with the overall strategy of the company. Some writers compare it with war, saying that the options are:

- **Deter:** Create barriers through contracts, copyright, licensing, trade agreements, agents; Exploit advantages of contacts, location, economy of scale, flexibility; Seek alliances
- **Attack:** Head on / flank through price, promotion, technology or marketing
- **Defend:** Customer database or network.

Competition forces your business to become a 'lean, mean, fighting machine'.

The second question is who are your competitors. We'll look more closely at this in *Marketing* a few pages on but, for now, remember than your competition may not just be local but may come from abroad, no matter how "local" your own business may be.

An information system

Part of being competitive is developing a system that constantly collects information about your competitors and about business trends generally. (See *Market Research* in **READY** and the previous section *Innovation*.)

Now answer the questions in the checklist below.

What types of decisions are you called on to make regularly?
What type of information do you need to make these decisions?
What type of information do you get regularly?
What type of information would you like to get that you are not getting now?
On which topics would you like to be kept informed?
What do you think would be the four most helpful improvements that could be made to your current information system?
Source: PLATO

Benchmarking

To assess how competitive your business is you need a benchmark. The most obvious benchmark is your competitors. Study them and score how they are performing on criteria that are important to the market and customers (see your earlier research). Identify areas in which:

- Your business is stronger
- Your business is weaker
- You can learn from your competitors
- Your business needs to improve
- Your competitors are developing and which you are ignoring.

Take all these factors into consideration as you write your business plan.

MARKETING

Since this workbook was first published, marketing has changed fundamentally in some respects and has stayed the same in others. Image and branding are still important, but social media has closed the gap between the two. Your reputation *is* your image. Social media is word-of-mouth on steroids. The customer experience determines the brand – which means an opportunity for you. You start with a blank sheet.

But still, the philosophy behind marketing is to satisfy the needs of every customer as best you can while making a profit. The whole idea is that if you make your clients happy they will buy from you – not just once, but again and again. This section will take you through the stages in developing a marketing plan.

TOO SMALL FOR A MARKETING DEPARTMENT?

Whether you have a marketing department or not, marketing involves decisions about:
- The product itself
- Price
- Customer service levels
- Physical distribution
- Advertising
- Sales
- The sales force
- Information about markets.

How do you decide on these?

MARKET RESEARCH

Your market research should have defined the customers the business is going to target. If not, go back to the *Market Research* section in **READY** and do more research on potential clients. Write down your answers to the questions below.

YOUR CUSTOMERS / TARGET GROUPS

Who are they?
Where are they located?
Can they be put in a social class and, if so, which class?
How do they spend their money?
Where do they spend their money?
Where do they socialise?
What do they read?
Where do they go online?
What do they watch on TV?
What do they listen to on radio?
Who forms their opinions?

The central idea of marketing is of a matching between a company's capabilities and the wants of customers in order to achieve the objectives of both parties.
MALCOLM MCDONALD, Marketing author

Business has only two functions: marketing and innovation.
PETER F DRUCKER, Management author

If it doesn't exist, it's a market opportunity.
VERN ROBURN

The outcome of any serious research can only be to make two questions grow where only one grew before.
THORSTEIN VEBLEN

Find out what elements in your service or product are most important to them. To understand fully your customers' needs, make sure to clarify exactly what the customer means by probing until you are clear what their real needs are. For example, if customers say they want "Total quality", ask "What do you mean by that?". When they answer "Quick response", you ask "What do you mean by quick response?". After asking "What do you mean?" a few times, you will establish their real need.

KEY PRODUCT / SERVICE ELEMENTS

Write down the five elements of your product / service that are most important to your customers:

1.
2.
3.
4.
5.

METRICS

Market research is not a one-off process – it's ongoing. Increasingly, start-ups are becoming more and more data-driven. You need to develop a dash-board with a number of key metrics that matter to you and your business.

Here are examples of metrics that successful start-ups use:

- Annual revenue per user (ARPU)
- Average transaction value (ATV)
- Break-even point
- Cost per download (CPD)
- Customer acquisition cost (CAC): The price you need to pay for someone to buy your product or service – this needs to be less (much less!) than the customer's LTV
- Life time value (LTV) of customer
- Revenue per employee

Also consider:

- **Retention:** Users coming back and buying your product / service multiple times
- **Referral:** Users who love your product / service so much they refer others to it

which then lead to your viral coefficient: $K = X \times Y \times Z$, where X is the percentage of users who refer or invite other clients, Y is the average number of people they invite (over a specific period of time) and Z is the percentage of people invited who buy.

You also need to measure your sale process in particular, Time to sell – in other words, how long does it take to close a sale from first contact to receiving money in your bank account.

I am the world's worst salesman. Therefore, I must make it easy for people to buy.
FW WOOLWORTH

Consumers are statistics. Customers are people.
STANLEY MARCUS

Ultimately the only metric that counts is sales. Once you start your business, you will be selling all day every day for the rest of your life! Do you think you can reach your break-even targets with the image and marketing plan? What sales do you need per day, every day?

COMPETITION

A competitor is a business that provides the same goods or services as yours or an alternative to your products / services.

Some competitors are obvious: a train company competes with private cars for journeys between cities – but another competitor might be online meeting software that allows businesspeople to "meet" without travelling. So think broadly about your actual – and potential – competitors.

Your competition can be local, national or, increasingly, international. Use the questions in the panel below to identify and assess your competitors.

YOUR COMPETITORS

What are the alternatives for your products or services?
Who makes / sells these alternatives?
What range of products or services do they have?
What kind of choices do they offer customers?
How broad is their range?
What are their target groups?
What are their future prospects?
What are they good at and what are they not so good at?

IMAGE

As markets are becoming more competitive and businesses have the same access to technology and information, image is increasingly important as a way to distinguish your business from the competition.

You should now decide what image you want your business to convey to your customers. For example, you may want your business / office / practice / shop / website to appear:

• Practical, simple and objective

• Exclusive, high value and durable

• Modern, new and trend-setting

• Personal, multi-faceted and results-oriented.

Consider your position statement in your strategic box again. What image do you want to project? Express it as colours, animals, book titles, movies, actors, music or locations. That should clarify what you want to project and what will resonate with your target audience

What image do you want to present?
Why?
How does this link back to your customers / target group?
How do you plan to achieve this image?

Once you have chosen an image, make sure it is expressed in all aspects of your business. Think about your business' image in these areas. Tick the ones you will use:

- Office / shop interior
- Pricing
- Name
- Business stationery
- Brochures
- Website
- Social media
- Packaging
- Quality

- Business plan
- Advertising
- Correspondence
- Service
- Telephone answering
- Presentation
- Promotion
- Selling
- Employees.

Once you have chosen the image you want to present to your customers, you should remain committed to it in the long term. See it as an investment in the future of your business.

Image needs to be maintained and should be checked on a regular basis with the reputation your business actually has. What perception do you want to project (= image)? And what is the image of your business that your customers have (= reputation)? Reputation is more important than image.

THE 4Ps OF THE MARKETING MIX

To market your product and project your image, you should use a mix of techniques and tools to get the best effect, depending on your product / service and the customers you are targeting.

If you sell physical products, you should use the classic 4Ps of the marketing:
- Product
- Price
- Place
- Promotion.

Recognising that selling services was different from selling products, marketing theorists extended the marketing mix to include the 3Ps of service:
- People
- Physical evidence
- Process.

Increasingly, the lines between product selling and services selling is blurring.

Within Promotion, we will look closely at Advertising, Personal Selling, Public Relations, Digital and Customer Service.

PRODUCT

For most customers, a product is not only the product itself (the core), but also the services and intangibles that surround it (the product surround). For example, a pub sells pints of beer (core) and quick service and atmosphere (surround); a clothes shop sells clothing and appearance or personal image, a flower shop sells plants and flowers and ambience in the house. What do you sell? What do your customers REALLY buy when they buy from you?

The customer also wants a choice. What you have to offer should consist of a range, a selection of choices, products that complement each other and make it attractive for the customer to come and buy. A pub also sells meals, a clothes shop also sells accessories, a flower shop also sells earthenware. What range of choices do you give your customers?

Customers also want to know what extras come with your product. What do you do that the others do not do? Think about packaging, service, personal attention, brand content, originality, authenticity, creativity and so on. What extras do you offer?

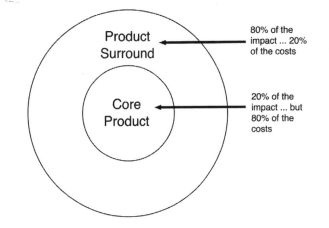

YOUR PRODUCT

Describe briefly the product(s) you want to launch:
Describe your product's value to the customer:
Describe your product's core:
Describe your product's surround:
What choices do you offer your customers?
What extras do you offer compared to the competition?

PRICE

Pricing is important for several reasons:

- The price you charge will determine your margins and, in the end, your own salary
- Price is also closely associated with the quality and credibility of your product or service
- Once you have established your price, it is very difficult to increase it without losing customers.

To establish your price, it is important to know what your customers are used to paying, and what they are prepared to pay (see the panel). (At this stage, price has nothing to do with cost – that comes later!)

You need to be well informed about competitors' prices. Sometimes prices are prescribed or recommended by industry organisations or professional associations. You can always deviate from established prices by means of special offers, discounts, reductions in rates, etc.

But be careful when researching price. You need to listen VERY carefully to what people say and how they say it. If your pricing is way out of line, people will tell you quickly. But, if it's a little dear, and they don't want to suggest that they can't afford it, they may say the price is fine. You will only find out that it's not fine when you can't sell the product / service. You must also bear in mind that anyone who intends buying a product or service is unlikely to tell you if it is too cheap. Tread carefully!

When you sell a product, you have something tangible to show the customer. With services, you have nothing to show until you have done the work – and sometimes not even then. If you offer a service, when you agree a price it is a good idea to write down for yourself exactly what your customer can expect – for example:

- Details of your service
- The time you will need complete the service
- The time when the service will start
- The price
- The agreed method (and time) of payment
- Whether the cost of materials is included
- Whether other expenses (travel to the customer's location, for example) are included.

The key to pricing services (and products too) is to understand the value that the customer places on the outcome. In a B2B environment, there is always a number: airports know what it costs them if a runway is closed due to snow; if you can save them 10 minutes more than your competitors in clearing it after a snowfall, they can easily put a value on that extra 10 minutes.

Get the confidence of the public and you will have no difficulty getting their patronage ... Remember always that the recollection of quality remains long after the price is forgotten.
H GEORGE SELFRIDGE, retailer

Price: Value plus a reasonable sum for the wear and tear on conscience in demanding it.
AMBROSE BIERCE, US Humorist

Almost anything on earth can be manufactured a little less well and be sold for a little less money. And those who are only interested in price are the main victims of this rule.
JOHN RUSKIN, Philosopher

In B2C, there are more emotions involved so the price you can charge is not always based rationally – which presents both opportunities and challenges. For example, in a B2B situation, when changing a car, there's a simple cost-benefit analysis: the cost of the new car against the savings from better fuel efficiency, etc. over the old car; in a B2C situation, sometimes the clincher may be a free upgrade to a better in-car entertainment system or having the latest number-plate to impress the neighbours!

There's always a tendency for start-ups to undercharge – our advice is to maximise price, consistent with your positioning and profitability. This means that you also need to look at price in the context of cost. There is no point selling lots of a product if you are losing money on it! Work through the questions below to determine your pricing strategy.

Note that if your customers are online, they can easily compare prices with other suppliers. How will this affect your pricing strategy?

YOUR PRICE

What are customers accustomed to paying already?
What are your competitors' prices (average)?
What is your price?
How is your price made up?
- Materials
- Time
- Machine cost
- Other product-related costs
- Cost of making a sale
- Total costs
- Break-even point
- Profit margin
- Selling price

Will you offer discounts? (If Yes, what kind of discount?)
Will you give special offers? (If Yes, what will they be?)

PLACE

Place means the location where your business will be established – offline and online.

Important questions to ask include:
- What will the customer see and experience when he or she visits your business offline or online?
- How easy is it to find you offline or online?
- Where are you physically situated (shopping area, a hotel or restaurant district, an office centre, in the centre or in the outskirts of town, etc.)?
- What draws customers to your location / website?

- Do you provide a location map for your customers on your website? Do you need to?

Channels of distribution

You need to understand the channels of distribution that you will be using for your product. Each industry is different and fortunes have been made (and lost) on changes to the channels of distribution. Look at how Apple has changed the way people buy music – and how the music companies have been unable to do the same. The right choice of channels can transform a business.

CHANNELS OF DISTRIBUTION

ORIGINATING PRODUCER				
⇩	⇩	⇩	⇩	⇩
⇩	⇩	⇩	Agent	⇩
⇩	⇩	⇩	⇩	⇩
⇩	⇩	Wholesaler	Wholesaler	⇩
⇩	⇩	⇩	⇩	⇩
⇩	Retailer	Retailer	Retailer	Post Office
⇩	⇩	⇩	⇩	⇩
CUSTOMER				

The diagram above summarises the main channels for physical products and the stages within them. The fewer stages, the lower the distribution cost – which is why lots of businesses try to cut out the middleman. On the other hand, the middleman provides a useful service – holding stock, sourcing customers, advising on market conditions – and cannot always be dispensed with. You need to balance distribution costs with promotion costs. Very often, sales channels with low distribution costs have high promotion costs.

Consider also alternatives to the traditional channels above that are making huge changes in the way people buy. How will they impact your business?

DISTRIBUTION CHECKLIST

What distribution system are you considering?
Why?
What do your competitors do?
Where are the weaknesses in your system?
How can they be corrected?

To understand channels in an online context, look at Brian Solis' Conversation Prism (**www.conversationprism.com**), which shows how rich and complicated social media is.

Distribution is everything. 80% of all buying decisions are researched online – 'moment marketing' is here. You need to be in the right place when potential customers are considering buying; you need to be in the right place when they buy; and you need to be able to deliver fast, if not instantly. Traditional models of doing business are changing and the routes to market are getting shorter. You need to consider digital distribution. You need to study the models in your sector and where they are going.

PROMOTION

This is the stage when you begin to develop your marketing plan. It is a mistake to think that marketing begins and ends with advertising. Although often the most visible part of marketing, advertising is just a part of the promotion plan, and it is therefore only one of the means of promotion, which include:

- Digital
- Direct mail
- Personal selling
- Public relations
- Publicity and advertising.

Each will be covered in more detail later, but below is a brief summary to set the context.

Digital

At a minimum, you will need a web presence and you should pick at least one social media channel through which to communicate with your clients. Here are the most obvious ones:

- Text messaging
- E-mail
- Facebook
- LinkedIn
- Google Plus
- Twitter
- Snapchat
- Pinterest
- Other ...

Digital allows you the extend your marketing reach. The minute you go online, you have access to a multi-billion people market-place. But so does every one of your competitors. Which is why you need to stand out. And here, all the marketing tools apply –

with an increased emphasis on storytelling, authenticity, passion and purpose as the battleground in which to compete. Technology, digital and quality are a given, what is the added value or not-to-copy part of your business?

Direct mail

Use a database of the names and addresses of the customers within your target groups to send a sales letter or brochure or email. Make it easy for the customer to respond. Where you can, follow up by phone.

Personal selling

The final target is selling your product. In most cases, you are the person who is going to sell. So, you must:
- Prepare your sales talk well
- Write down your customers' buying motives and also the reasons why they might not buy
- Think of reasons to counter those objections.

For example, Apple employees are taught specifically not to persuade, but rather to help customers solve problems or address needs and aspirations. "Your job is to understand all of your customers' needs", they are told. In fact, Apple sales employees receive no sales commissions and have no sales quotas. In the training manuals, Apple lays out its 'steps of service', using the acronym APPLE (what else?):
- **Approach** customers with a personalized warm welcome
- **Probe** politely to understand all the customer's needs
- **Present** a solution for the customer to take home today
- **Listen** for and resolve any issues or concerns
- **End** with a fond farewell and an invitation to return.

Public relations (PR)

PR embraces all the activities you undertake to get positive attention for your business among the public in general. Good PR creates a positive image for your business and helps to ensure that people recognise and remember your business. Good PR is also useful for your contacts with your suppliers. If you need a quick delivery, a special order or a credit, try to make sure that your supplier will go out of their way to help you. The same applies for your neighbours, local authority, etc. Good PR will also lead to free publicity.

The key steps in advertising are:
- Use the image you developed earlier as the basis for your ads
- Look for an aspect of your business' image that can be represented graphically
- Always emphasise the advantages for the customer

- Remain credible and trustworthy
- Gain attention with a headline and give sufficient information
- Raise interest with a special offer
- Motivate your public to come and buy
- Stimulate action by including something that must be returned, an invitation, an opening, special sales days, discount coupon valid until (date).

Methods of promotion

There are hundreds of ways of promoting your business and the products / services you offer. Try some of these:
- Advertise online
- Publish content online
- Engage in social media
- Advertise in a newspaper or magazine aimed at your target group
- Advertisement or entry in the Golden Pages (a basic line entry is free of charge)
- Design and print brochures that can be delivered house-to-house with the newspaper delivery or deliver them yourself; distribute brochures during large meetings or conferences, at markets, in the street, to customers, etc.
- Have posters made and hang them strategically
- Direct mail – send sales letters directly to potential customers and your existing customers for whom you have an address
- Participation in trade exhibitions, markets, hiring a stand at a conference. You will gain the opportunity here to demonstrate your products. Remember you will need brochures to distribute. You can also make a special exhibition offer
- Make up your front window display according to a theme.

In practice, you will probably choose a combination of methods to make up your promotion mix.

ADVERTISING

Advertising is a way of communicating your product or service. Based on your market research, you know who your target groups are and how to reach them. What do you want your advertising to achieve:
- Sales?
- Awareness?
- Image?
- Name recognition?
- Introduce new product / service?

The codfish lays ten thousand eggs,
The humble hen just one.
The codfish never cackles
To tell you when she's done.
And so we scorn the codfish
While the humble hen we prize,
Which only goes to show you
That it pays to advertise.
ANON

Doing business without advertising is like winking at a girl across a darkened room: You know what you are doing but no one else does.
ANON

Give them quality. That's the best kind of advertising.
MILTON HERSHEY

When business is good, it pays to advertise; when business is bad, you've got to advertise.
ANON

Advertising: The education of the public as to who you are, where you are, and what you have to offer in the way of skill, talent or commodity.
FRANK MCKINNEY HUBBARD, US humorist

51

Go back to your market research. Remind yourself of your customers' buying motives. Then decide which of your product's / service's features meet these motives and should be emphasised in your advertising.

Take control!

Offline or online, ask for a 'media pack'. This will tell you not only the rates, but who the visitors / readers / listeners / viewers are, how many they are, what income groups they are in, etc. You need this information in order to decide whether a vehicle is suitable.

Nowadays, it probably more sense to start with some simple online marketing – some keywords and SEO – before looking at offline advertising.

Don't be pressurised into advertising, either in the wrong place or at the wrong time. Most ad salespeople are on commission. They want you to buy NOW! and will give you 'special discounts' – if you decide today. Don't do it until you are ready.

Don't be fooled by price either. Yes, one magazine charges €500 for a half-page against €300 for a full page in another newspaper – but the first goes to 20,000 of your core customers whereas the other really doesn't cover your market at all. Which is better value?

When you have placed your ads, measure the response. Unless you do this, you will never know whether your advertising works. There is a famous advertising story of an American car manufacturer that advertised for a year in a well-respected national magazine. At the end of the year, the company found that people who had not read the magazine bought more of their cars than did readers of the magazine. Their advertising was effectively UN-selling the cars!

Measurability is a key attraction of online advertising (the other attraction is that online is probably where many, if not most, of your customers look for information before they buy).

If it is appropriate, place a 'call to action' ("Call us now for special offer details" or "Register for ezine") on your advertisement. Record the number of responses you get from each ad. This will save you from advertising in the wrong places in future.

Writing advertisements

Writing advertisements is an art. It looks simple but it is, in fact, very hard. Keep these words by David Ogilvy, founder of Ogilvy & Mather, one of the world's largest advertising agencies, in mind: "I do not regard advertising as entertainment or as an art form, but as a medium of information. When I write an advertisement, I don't want you to tell me you find it 'creative'. I want you to find it so interesting that *you buy the product*".

The secret is to keep it simple. Be direct. Explain what you are selling, its benefits to the customer, and where they can get it.

Use your logo

If your business has a strong visual appeal, design a logo. Use it as widely as you can. Use it on every page of your website, on emails, envelopes, T-shirts, posters or promotional gifts.

Make sure that wherever they go, your target customers are always aware that your business exists.

PERSONAL SELLING

For lots of people, selling still has a negative connotation – the image of a slick sales person pushing products onto a customer.

Not anymore. Modern-day selling is about partnership and communication. It is important to build a relationship with your customers. The customer must trust and respect you.

Try to build a database with the names and addresses of your customers. Try to memorise the names of your customers, remember what they bought the last time, or what they asked about last time. Again, get as much information as you can about your customers' hobbies, family situation, job, etc. Use that information when you next talk to them. The following checklists may be helpful to you in developing your personal selling techniques.

All of the above is wasted if you do not get sales appointments with the right people. Realise that nine out of 10 appointments result in a "No". Sure, if you get nine Nos, you also get one "Yes". But, if you qualify leads early, you reduce the number of "Nos" for each "Yes".

> To sell no matter what, no matter how, to no matter whom; behold in these words the whole diplomacy of the peasant at the fair.
> **JOSEPH ROUX (1834-1905)**

> The average salesperson spends less than 25% of their time face-to-face with their clients. Personally, I spend 90%. That's the only way to make money in sales.
> **EDNA LARSEN**

> To open a shop is easy, to keep it open is an art.
> **CONFUCIUS**

WHEN SELLING

Are you prepared?
Do you know your customers' needs? (Ask lots of questions)
Do you listen?
Are you clear in your language? (No jargon!)
Do you talk about benefits instead of the product?
Do you have answers to your customers' objections? (What are their objections?)
Do you know when to close the sale?
Are you persistent? (Do not give up)

THINGS TO ASK YOURSELF BEFORE YOU START SELLING

Do you know enough about the product?
What is the product's value to the customer?
What is the product core?
What is the product surround?
Are you talking to the right person, who has both the money and the decision-making power to buy?
Who are:
- The recommenders?
- The influencers?
- The supporters?
- The deciders?

Do you know what the customer wants?
Does what he / she wants fit with what he needs?
Why does the customer want it?
Have you had any previous experience with the customer?
Has the customer had experience with your competition?
Who is the end user of your product?
How will your product be used?
How will the customer's life be better or easier after he / she uses your product?

Selling – day in, day out, year in, year out – is the most underestimated element in business, because without sales, there is no business!

PUBLIC RELATIONS

Public relations (PR) is not just about getting your business in the media. Public relations is exactly what it says: Building a relationship with the public.

Let's first define public. From the perspective of where your business is physically located, it includes:
- Neighbours
- The neighbourhood
- The local community.

Internally, it includes staff and suppliers.

Online, it includes bloggers, thought-leaders and opinion-formers.

In a wider context, public includes:
- Colleagues
- Unions and trade organisations
- Government (local, regional, national)
- Politicians
- Consumer groups
- Financial institutions.

PR builds and maintains a good reputation. If your business is well-regarded, your marketing mix will be strengthened and it will be easier to influence people or get things done (planning permission, recruiting staff, word-of-mouth sales, etc.)

It goes back to your mission statement and what social profile you want to project. You must decide which groups you want to maintain a positive relationship with and how you plan to do this. Keep it practical and within your means (money and time).

Local media are always looking for news. If you have good news about your business, make sure you let them know. Build a profile for yourself and your business through your local media outlets.

And while the relationship you build will not protect you totally when bad news must be reported, it means the reporter knows and trusts you already and may go out of their way to check facts with you before going to print.

PUBLIC RELATIONS CHECKLIST	
Neighbours – Who are they?	
• Local banks?	☐ YES ☐ NO
• Local politicians?	☐ YES ☐ NO
• Local authority?	☐ YES ☐ NO
• Local media?	☐ YES ☐ NO
• Trade organisations?	☐ YES ☐ NO
• Unions?	☐ YES ☐ NO
• State agencies?	☐ YES ☐ NO
• Other?	☐ YES ☐ NO
How will you reach them:	
• Sponsorship?	☐ YES ☐ NO
• Press releases?	☐ YES ☐ NO
• Visits / Open Days?	☐ YES ☐ NO
• Information / newsletter?	☐ YES ☐ NO
• Profile in local media?	☐ YES ☐ NO
• Donate your services for a worthy cause?	☐ YES ☐ NO

CUSTOMER SERVICE

Businesses spend a lot of money on attracting new customers. But it is cheaper to keep your existing customers than to find new ones.

Loyal customers:

- Spend more money with you than other customers
- Bring in new customers (through word-of-mouth recommendations)
- Cost less than acquiring new customers.

Use the panel on the next page to calculate the lifetime value of one of your customers.

THE IMPORTANCE OF CUSTOMER LOYALTY – CALCULATE THE LIFETIME VALUE OF A CUSTOMER

Average sale value per customer
multiplied by
Number of sales per year per customer
=
Total sales value per year per customer
multiplied by
Number of years customer buys from you
= Gross lifetime sales value per customer

Plus, if every satisfied customer tells one or two other people and they become customers, look how fast your sales will grow!

What steps will you take to keep your customers loyal to your business:

- Regular visits?
- Regular telephone contact?
- Regular direct mail / email contact?
- Regular evaluation of your business' performance in meeting their needs?
- Interviews with customers whose business you have lost to find out why this happened?

One way of creating and keeping loyal customers is through customer service – not just any old customer service but through superb world-class customer service. World-class? Why not? Where's the competition? When did you last get service from any business that was so good that you would recommend someone else to use them? When did you last get service so good that you noticed?

Customer service involves:

- Doing what you promised the customer
- Willingness to help
- Providing prompt service
- Well-trained staff
- Individual attention
- Little things which make the difference.

The fact that you have only a small business makes no difference – in fact, it makes it easier for you to be close to the customer.

Research shows that businesses that provide top class customer service experience:

- Improvements in morale (reducing staff costs)
- Lower staff turnover (reducing recruitment costs)
- Longer customer retention (up to 50% longer)
- More repeat business (20% to 40% lower selling costs)
- More referrals (20% to 40% lower promotional costs)
- Higher prices (7% to 12% higher)

If you mean to profit, learn to please.
CHARLES CHURCHILL

Good service isn't a mystery – employ nice people.
KEN McCULLOCK, One Devonshire Gardens Hotel, Glasgow

56

- Increased margins (7% to 17% more profit).

Calculate the difference all of these (or even one or two of them) would make to your profits. Then decide how you are going to put customer service into action in your business.

EXPORT

It may appear strange to be considering exporting when you haven't even got your business up and running but many Irish businesses have to consider exporting at an earlier stage in their development than is usual in other bigger countries. Use the checklist to help you plan your export strategy.

EXPORT CHECKLIST

How specific are your plans?

Are they an integral part of your business plan and strategy for the business?

Which products or services do you want to export to?

Which countries do you want to export to and in which order of priority?

What is your target market / segments within the market?

Have you done desk research on your export markets?

Have you actually visited the countries involved?

Do you have sales experience in your proposed export markets?

Do you have the language skills needed?

Have you organised your administration for foreign payments and customs / excise regulations?

Are you familiar with the regulations relating to your products / services in your export markets?

Does your product or service need adjustment for safety, environment, quality, packaging, taste, fashion, culture or language?

Is your price, after calculation of the extra costs involved in exporting, still competitive?

What are your turnover targets: per country, per market, per segment?

Do you have enough time available to build and develop the export market?

Who will be responsible for marketing and sales abroad?

Is your organisation, from telephonist to after sales, ready and prepared for export and dealing internationally?

Can your business cope with the demands of foreign markets: delivery times, transport, quantities?

Which channels are you planning to use in your export markets?

Do you have the right promotion and instruction materials?

Are your term and conditions, contracts, quotes, etc. translated and adjusted to your export markets?

MARKETING PLAN

At this stage, you should have enough information to be able to develop an outline marketing plan. Just as marketing is the heart of your business, so your marketing plan is the heart of your business plan.

As shown in the diagram, your plan should start with the mission statement, include your business and personal objectives and then summarise the results of your market research. The SWOT analysis, based on the market research, leads to assumptions, which in turn lead to the definition of targets and strategies.

Sales estimates may not be acceptable first time around, so alternatives may need to be considered.

Sales estimates can be difficult for a start-up, since you have no track-record or experience to base them on. Try to support your sales estimates with as much hard evidence – forward orders, etc. – as you can.

Once sales estimates have been agreed, the budgeting process can begin – and then work begins in earnest on putting the plan into action.

Note that the diagram also includes a measurement and review loop.

Marketing is a constant process.

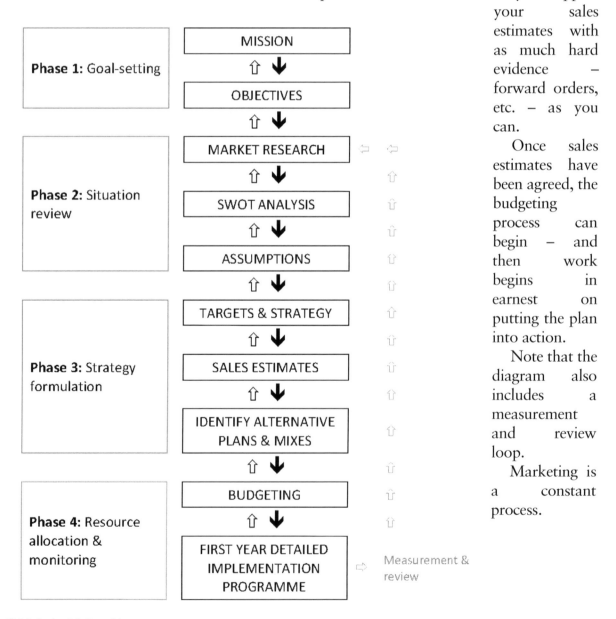

© Malcolm McDonald

DIGITAL

Digital and the power of the Internet have significant benefits to offer small businesses. But the Internet will not make you a millionaire overnight. It is not a magic wand. You need a good understanding of your business model and where digital might fit.

Don't get bogged down – or put off – by the technology. As any good techie will tell you, it is not the technology that is the key to success, but how you use the available technology.

You must have a website

A website offers a window onto a global networked marketplace, making it easy for you to reach customers whom you would probably never have considered targeting. For example, Oak Tree Press, publisher of this workbook, has a website (**www.SuccessStore.com**), which reaches customers around the world, through an online catalogue.

But before you rush into setting up your own website, stop and think. Ask yourself:

- **Is your business suitable?** Are you providing goods or services that can be delivered easily world-wide (or, at least, remotely from your present location)? Or, if not, can you attract customers to come to you (hotel, tourist resort)?

- **Are your customers (and potential customers) connected to the Internet?** Think carefully about what you need to invest; simple e-mail may be sufficient.

- **Are you clear about what you are trying to do?** A website can be used for a number of purposes (often simultaneously), including providing product support to existing customers, providing product information to potential customers, selling online, identifying prospects, receiving feedback from customers, advertising your business' existence, capability and excellence. Which are you doing?

- **Can you afford it – time-wise?** Establishing a site is only the first step. You must then update it regularly. How often depends on your business and the web traffic you generate. Once a month is a good target to aim for. But it all takes time

- **Can you afford it – money-wise?** Setting up a website costs money. Not a lot, to be sure, but it all adds up.

Finally, ask yourself: Can you afford NOT to have a website?

Security

Issues in relation to security on the web include:

- **Safety:** Whether sensitive information (credit card details, for example) is protected while it is being sent from the user's computer to the web server and onwards (if applicable)

In Internet business, profitability is for wimps. It means your business plan wasn't aggressive enough.
DOONESBURY

It's working if it makes the till ring.
DES KENNY, Kenny's Bookshop, Galway

The golden rule of complying with e-commerce law is: Be transparent! By being completely and fully transparent about who you are, what you are doing and how you will serve your customer, you will find that you are not only staying on the right side of the law but you are also keeping your customers happy.
CORINNA SCHULZE and JEFFREY BAUMGARTNER, *Don't Panic: Do E-commerce*

- **Trust:** Whether commitments made on the web will be honoured (for example, will goods bought and paid for online be dispatched?)
- **Privacy:** Whether there are restrictions on the access to, and use of, personal information (for example, age or financial status) provided by a user as part of a web transaction (see Trading Laws for more).

Other issues

Other issues in relation to selling online include:

- **Currency:** Good marketing practice suggests you offer products for sale in your customers' currency (usually US $ on the Web). This raises issues because of fluctuating exchange rates / differing price points.

- **Delivery:** Can you meet customers' expectations for delivery? After all, if they can find your product and order it in a few minutes, why must they wait for several weeks while it travels to them?

- **Shipping costs:** Who bears shipping costs? You will find that postage of bulky items overseas is expensive – and express couriers are not cheap.

TEN RULES FOR A SUCCESSFUL B2C E-COMMERCE SITE

Keep it simple.
Make it fast.
Minimise friction.
Build trust.
Create communities.
Think globally.
Make paying / shipping easy.
Let the world know.
Measure everything.
Source: Adapted from Marco Argenti & Efrim Boritz

PRODUCTS & PRODUCTION

Production is deliberately placed AFTER marketing in this guide because, too often, in the real world, production comes before marketing – to the detriment of the business.

This section will help you think through what you should be doing. Start by writing down the answers to the questions below.

o Understand your production process

YOUR PRODUCTS / SERVICES		
Products / services	Description	Price
A		
B		
C		

Describe your production process. Draw a flowchart on a separate page, if necessary.

What experience do you have with this process?

Are you involved with (or will you be using) new techniques or new products in your production processes? ☐ YES ☐ NO

If Yes, are you receiving assistance from experts? ☐ YES ☐ NO

If Yes, who are they and how are they engaged?

Copy this section into your business plan, pages 144 and 148.

Develop standards

To ensure efficient production, it might be worthwhile developing procedures and measuring your activities so that you can standardise your approach. Standards should enable you to:

- Do the job the easiest (and safest) way
- Prevent errors from (re-)occurring
- Have a benchmark to measure and improve against
- Have objectives to work against
- Provide a basis to train your future staff
- Preserve the knowledge and experience you are developing as you go along.

In the same way as you analysed your idea in the **READY** chapter, you should now put your production process under the microscope. Use the panel on the next page to help you.

Then read widely on production and manufacturing techniques, according to your needs.

Digital

Digital has become a catchphrase for a lot of things in business. It is a reference to social media, but also a reference to digital as a way to design your business and / or a way to deliver your product or service. The rule should be that everything that can be digitised, should be digitised.

The panel records your production process. Look at it closely. Ask:
- Where are there gaps?
- Where are there inefficiencies?
- Where is there duplication of work?
- Where is there work that could be sub-contracted out more effectively?
- How could the process be improved?
- Are there any capacity constraints or bottle-necks? How can these be overcome?
- How do you propose to keep your product up-to-date?
- What parts of your product can be recycled?
- How could your product be re-designed so that more parts could be recycled? At what cost?
- Is your product protected by patent?
- What quality assurance systems have you in place? How do they operate?
- Have your systems been certified by an external body?

Break down your customer's 'journey' from first awareness of need (or potential need) to the conclusion of purchase and enjoyment of your product. Identify what technology you can use for each part. Look at each element and ask:
- Can it be digitized?
- Can it be outsourced?
- Can it be scaled?

Use of the Internet also can facilitate a reduction in transaction costs. Some estimates suggest that the use of a B2B exchange could cut transaction costs by 90% for some businesses. Even allowing for exaggeration, there is clearly an enormous potential for cost reductions in many areas of business, which will bring benefits to the economy, individual businesses and ultimately to the consumer.

'Friction' – roadblocks and difficulties on the path to purchase – is the reason why you receive negative feedback. Digital helps you to remove that friction. The most usual friction points are the website and in particular the webshop (how many clicks is your customer away from ordering?), delivery, knowing / learning how to use your product / service, customer service and customer engagement.

What are the friction points? For each, ask:
- Can it be done quicker?
- Can it be done easier (for the customer, but perhaps also for you)?
- Are you applying design thinking?

Applying some digital / design thinking might transform your business idea.

STAFF

HOW MANY STAFF?

At an early stage, you need to begin to estimate how many staff you may need and how this number will grow – and where you will recruit staff from. There's not much point planning expansion if you can't get the people to do the work.

Use the panel below to estimate your initial staff numbers and how you see this developing within the first 12 months and within the first three years.

These figures will help you to develop your financial projections (see page 116) and in making applications for employment grants, if you are eligible.

Remember that salary is not the only cost in employing someone. PRSI must be paid on their earnings (see *Taxation*); they may be entitled to bonuses, commissions, etc.; they will need training – and there will be other costs you have not thought of.

(see page 116)

OBJECTIVES
o Be aware of recruitment sources and techniques
o Be aware of employment legislation
o Be aware of staff management techniques

Future staffing	Management	Production	Sales	Marketing	Administration	Other
+12 months						
+ 3 years						

STAFFING PLAN

Initially, how will your staffing be organised?
- You alone, while holding another wage-earning position
- You alone, full-time
- You and your partner, full-time
- You and your partner, part-time
- You and your business partner(s)
- You and your business partner(s) with employees at a wage?

How many employees full-time?
How many employees part-time?
How do you see this expanding?
Copy this section to your business plan, page 145.

Copy this section to your business plan, page 145.

All commercial operations can, in the final analysis, be summed up in three words: personnel, products, profits. Personnel comes first. Without a good team, it is impossible to expect anything from the other two.
LEE IACOCCA

The person who figures out how to harness the collective genius of his or her organisation is going to blow the competition away.
WALTER WRISTON

DELEGATING

Delegating is difficult for entrepreneurs.

Their whole business, their way of life, is built on their own vision. What should be done, when and how are all determined by the entrepreneur. And now parts of the business, even decisions, are to be handed over to someone else. Ouch! This is very often the way that entrepreneurs see delegating – in a negative light, as giving up control. But that's not delegating – that's giving up control!

Delegating is a specific sequence of techniques that empowers one person (the person to whom work is delegated) while freeing up the time of another (the person delegating). Delegation involves:

- **Defining the task:** In terms of resources available and outcome required, not in terms of method
- **Transferring a clear understanding:** To the person who is to do the work
- **Standing back and letting them do the work, while being available to help:** But only when asked
- **Careful, shared evaluation of the outcome.**

It is critical that achievement of the task is judged only in terms of the outcome – not the methods used to achieve it.

If you want a store-room tidied and products placed on shelves in alphabetical order, does it matter whether the person starts by finding all the most popular items first and putting them aside? Or that the alphabetical sequence starts left of the door, and not right? Or that he begins tidying at Z and not A? Just because it isn't done the way you would have done it does not make it wrong.

The important points in delegation are the task definition and the evaluation. You must sit down with the person after the task is complete and talk through what they achieved. Because you have more experience, you may know faster, better, cheaper ways of doing the task – but you should let the person identify these for themselves. If you tell them, they will never learn. Worse still, they will give up, saying to themselves "I did the job. Got the right result. But all the boss was concerned about was doing it his way".

The other difficulty that entrepreneurs have with delegation is a lack of recognition that their own drive differs from that of their employees. You will quite happily stay at work late into the night, work through weekends and bank holidays, but you cannot expect that your staff will always want to do the same. Good staff will be prepared to work on to get the job done – but not just for the sake of doing. You need to learn to motivate – and be reasonable in your demands.

DELEGATION

How much does your time cost?   €
(the standard calculation is 3 times salary, divided by 200 days,
divided again by 8 hours in a day = € per hour)
Do you really want to take work home in the evenings and
weekends?
What areas do you think you must deal with yourself?
What areas are most critical to the business?
What areas are you comfortable delegating to another person?
Delegate what to whom?
Develop a profile of the right person for each task you want to
delegate and match your staff to the profiles.

RECRUITING

Recruiting staff is a major stumbling block for many small businesses. It takes time and effort. But the results can have an enormous impact on your bottom line. Hire the right people, and you will have a strong staff who will move your company forward. But the wrong person will pull down morale, waste your time, and cost you more than just an extra salary.

The key steps are:
- Know what you're looking for
- Finding applicants
- Interviews.

Know what you're looking for

Before you begin looking for someone to fill a vacancy, you need to know what you're looking for. You should:

- **Create a detailed job description:** Write down the specific tasks you expect this employee to perform. Think about every detail. Then summarise and put the tasks in order of priority

- **Develop a list of skills required:** What skills are essential? What skills are merely desirable?

- **Decide what other things you want:** Specific educational background? Experience in a particular industry? What else is necessary for the person to develop in your company?

- **Think about personality:** You need people who share your vision and your standards.

- **Take a reality check:** Look at what you have written down. Which areas are priorities? Where are you willing to compromise? Will you get the person you want for the salary you are offering?

Finding applicants

Requirements defined, you now need to find people to meet them. Here are some suggestions:

- **Look online / use social media:** Your company's reputation and social reach, as well as its staff's connections, offer a unique population of potential recruits, who come recommended

- **Look in your files:** A visible and successful company will have people writing in looking for jobs, even though no vacancies are being advertised. If any of these people look promising, make time to meet and find out more about them. Then, when you need a particular mix of skills, you may find the perfect candidate in your files already

- **Ask your staff:** Your own staff may know someone with the right skills whom they would be happy to recommend (for a bonus, perhaps). And they will come with a built-in guarantee, since they won't want to let down the staff-member who sponsored them

- **Ask around:** Ask everyone you know (including customers and suppliers) whether they know anyone they would recommend. Have some background information available on the job ready to give out

- **Advertising:** Make it clear what you are looking for and write the ad to attract candidates. But make sure you have the time to handle a deluge of responses, if that happens

- **Use a recruitment agency:** A sensible route if you do not have the time or ability to screen applicants, but it can be expensive. Through their contacts, agencies can often find people whom you would otherwise not reach with an advertisement

- **Contact university / Institute of Technology career offices:** They are always looking for jobs for their graduates and will often circulate your listing free of charge or for a small fee

- **Job fairs:** An opportunity to give your company some visibility and talk to a variety of candidates in an unpressured environment

- **Non-traditional workers:** Don't overlook older or part-time workers or those with disabilities – they can be very capable and committed

- **Recruit abroad:** May be necessary where you face skills shortages (see below for more information).

Whatever route you choose, it is a good idea to insist that every candidate completes a standard application (see next chapter, **GO!**). Keep the form simple but make sure that you get all the information you need to decide whether a candidate has the skills you require for the specific position. Use the candidate's CV as a back-up.

Make a shortlist

Before you start looking at CVs or application forms, write out again a summary of the main points you are looking for in a candidate. Screen quickly looking for these – and only these. Put all applications that do not meet these criteria into a separate bundle. If you want, review them later to see whether they include any candidates you might want to keep for your files. Otherwise, remove them from consideration immediately. Write to them to say that you will not be calling them to interview – from the candidate's point of view, it's better to get bad news than not to hear at all and it's better to get it quickly, so they can concentrate their energies elsewhere.

Concentrate on the candidates who meet your criteria. Read their CVs again more carefully. Look for little things: gaps in employment, jobs that don't quite fit a career path, hobbies that don't sit well with the personality type you are looking for, inconsistencies and even, if the job involves written communication, misspellings and poor grammar.

Make a shortlist. Decide which candidates you want to interview and contact them to arrange dates and times. Although interview candidates should do their own research on your business before coming for interview, it is helpful to include some background information on your business with the letter confirming the interview.

Recruiting from abroad

Before deciding to recruit foreign workers, consider whether you can source staff locally, since overseas recruitment is usually more expensive when all costs are considered than local recruitment.

If it's necessary, you should know that:

- Workers from outside the EU or EEA (EU plus Norway, Liechtenstein and Iceland) require work permits
- Work permits are issued by the Department of Jobs, Enterprise and Innovation to either the employer or the employee
- There are a number of different kinds of work permits, the requirements for which change from time to time
- Visas may be required by some non-EU nationals
- All non-EU nationals resident in Ireland for more than 90 days must register with the Gardaí.

For up-to-date information on this constantly changing area, check the Department of Business, Enterprise and Innovation's website (**www.dbei.gov.ie**).

Interviewing

When interviewing, you only have a short time to find out all you need to make an informed decision about investing in someone who should become an asset to your business. Therefore:

- **Use an interview checklist:** Develop a list of points that you want to cover during the interview

- **Ask open-ended questions:** Avoid questions that can be answered "Yes" or "No"; instead use questions like *"Why did you like working in sales?"*, *"What are your strengths and weaknesses?"* or *"Why are you leaving your current job?"*

- **Ask unconventional questions:** See how candidates think (and how fast) by asking them questions they may not have prepared for. For example, *"Why shouldn't all staff be paid the same?"* or *"If you didn't have to work, what would you do with your time?"*

- **Find out what's important to the candidate:** What is he / she looking for: growth opportunities, regular hours, training, new responsibilities? Will he / she finish the job or just clock-watch?

- **Listen:** Spend 20% of the time talking and 80% listening. The purpose of the interview is to help you learn about the candidates, not to talk about yourself or your business

- **Interview more than once:** Use the first interview to find the top two or three candidates; use the second to make sure you choose the best

- **Involve other staff:** If you are particularly pleased with a candidate, let them meet some of your existing staff with whom they will be working. Get these staff-members' opinion

- **Check references:** Ask what the relationship between the candidate and their referee is. Confirm previous positions, responsibilities and achievements. Ask about working habits, ability to get along with others, problems, etc.

Be open with candidates. Tell them that you are interviewing others. Give them a date by which they can expect to hear from you – one way or the other. Be fair – keep to it.

INTERVIEW CHECKLIST

Candidate name:

Meets educational criteria?	☐ YES ☐ NO
Meets experience criteria?	☐ YES ☐ NO
Passed competence test?	☐ YES ☐ NO
Has essential skills?	☐ YES ☐ NO
Has desirable skills?	☐ YES ☐ NO
Has additional skills?	☐ YES ☐ NO
Good oral communication skills?	☐ YES ☐ NO
Good written communication skills?	☐ YES ☐ NO
Has foreign language skills?	☐ YES ☐ NO
Good personality?	☐ YES ☐ NO
Would fit in well with other staff?	☐ YES ☐ NO
Currently employed?	☐ YES ☐ NO
Notice period needed?	☐ YES ☐ NO
Clean driving licence?	☐ YES ☐ NO
Smoker?	☐ YES ☐ NO
Good health record?	☐ YES ☐ NO
Days off in past year?	☐ YES ☐ NO
Permission to contact referees?	☐ YES ☐ NO

The job offer

You should have already discussed the job offer with your ideal candidate at interview, before writing to offer the job – in some cases, you may make the offer at the interview and shake hands on a deal. Either way, you should write to the selected candidate and set out clearly:

- The job title and description
- The salary – how it is to be paid, and whether it includes overtime, bonuses, etc.
- The normal hours of work
- Holidays
- Period of notice required on resignation / dismissal
- Grievance procedures
- Any other 'house' rules.

Send two copies of this letter, both signed by you, and ask for one back, signed by the new appointee to signify their acceptance of the position on the terms offered.

EMPLOYMENT LEGISLATION

Note that there is a clear distinction, particularly for tax purposes, between employees and self-employed contractors. Check with the Department of Social Protection or the Revenue Commissioners.

By law, full-time employees are entitled to:

- A written contract of employment
- Minimum wages

- Equal pay for equal work
- Protection against discrimination
- Holidays and rest periods
- Maternity, adoptive and parental leave
- Trade union membership
- Minimum notice on termination of employment
- Protection against unfair dismissal
- Protection against redundancy, and minimum payments if it should occur.

A written contract of employment

Employees are entitled to a written statement of the terms of employment, within one month of requesting it (see sample in GO). This must set out:
- Details of the employment
- The dismissal procedure the employer will use
- Salary
- Deductions from salary.

Minimum wages

The National Minimum Wages Act, 2000 requires employers to pay experienced adult workers (those over 18, more than two years employed and not a trainee) a minimum average hourly rate. This rate is updated from time to time.

Equal pay for equal work

Where men and women perform similar work, under similar conditions, or requiring similar skills, or work of similar value or responsibility, they must be paid the same.

Equality Officers of the Labour Court have the right to enter premises, examine records and seek information where an equality claim is made.

Protection against discrimination

The *Employment Equality Acts, 1998-2015* ban discrimination on the basis of sex or marital status in:
- Recruitment
- Conditions of employment other than pay or pension (covered by equality legislation)
- Training and work experience
- Opportunities for promotions.

Holidays

Most employees are entitled to a minimum of 20 days annual leave, plus public holidays (8 each year). Legally, the 'holiday year' runs from 1 April to 31 March and pro-rata entitlements apply for periods of less than a year.

The *Organisation of Working Time Act, 1997* also requires that employees:

- Work no more than a 48-hour week, averaged over a 4, 6 or 12 month period as appropriate
- Have rest breaks while at work
- Have 11 hours rest in each 24-hour period
- Have one period of 24 hours rest per week, preceded by a daily rest period of 11 hours.

The Act applies to all workers, except Gardaí and the Defence Forces. Its general provisions may be varied by collective agreement.

Maternity leave

Regardless of length of service, a pregnant employee has the right to:

- Take up to 26 weeks paid and 16 weeks unpaid maternity leave
- Return to work, to her previous job or one of similar status, afterwards
- Reasonable time off for ante and post-natal care.

The Department of Social Protection pays her a pay-related Maternity Allowance for 26 weeks. The remaining 16 weeks maternity leave are unpaid. There is no obligation on the employer to pay any salary during maternity leave. The employee must give her employer four weeks written notice of her intention to take maternity leave and the dates of her leave. She must also give her employer four weeks written notice of her intention to return to work after maternity leave.

Paternity leave

New parents (other than the mother of the child) can get two weeks statutory paternity leave from employment or self-employment following the birth or adoption of a child on or after 1 September 2016.

Adoptive leave

A woman employee is entitled to 24 weeks paid and 16 weeks unpaid adoptive leave under much the same terms as maternity leave above. Similar leave is available to sole male adopters.

Parental leave

Both parents are entitled to up to 18 weeks unpaid leave to take care of a child up to eight years of age (up to 16 years of age in the case of a child with a long-term illness). This leave can be taken in a single block or two blocks of a minimum of six weeks, although other arrangements may be made by agreement with the employer, who must be informed in writing six weeks in advance. The *Parental Leave Act, 1998*, as amended by the *Parental Leave (Amendment) Act, 2006*, provides for paid *force majeure* leave of up to three days in a year or five days over three years on the sudden illness / injury of an immediate family member.

Trade union membership

The Irish *Constitution* is an employee's ultimate assurance of the right to form or to join a trade union. Union activities, in particular, disputes and their conduct, are covered by the *Industrial Relations Act, 1990*, which also established the Labour Relations Commission (now the Workplace Relations Commission).

Minimum notice on termination of employment

The *Minimum Notice to Terminate Employment Act, 1973*, applies to employees in continuous service for 13 weeks.

Protection against unfair dismissal

Where an employee has been employed for more than 12 months, he / she is deemed to have been unfairly dismissed unless the criteria for a fair dismissal laid down in the *Unfair Dismissals Act, 1977* have been met. Among other things, the Act requires that:

- The procedures for dismissal laid down by the employer be fair
- The procedures be operated fairly.

A short-term contract must be signed by both employee and employer and clearly state that the provisions of the 1977 Act do not apply, in order to be considered a valid reason for dismissal at the expiry of the contract term.

Protection against redundancy

Where redundancy is unavoidable, an employee is entitled to payment by the employer (or failing this, from the State). The amounts of the payments are set by law and vary according to age and length of service.

Part-time employees

Part-time workers do not have the same rights as full-time workers, although the *Worker Protection (Regular Part-time Employee) Act, 1991* extended some benefits of full-time working to 'regular' part-time employees, though not to 'casual' part-time employees (those with less than 13 weeks service not in regular or seasonal employment).

MANAGING STAFF

Businesses go through different stages of development and the management style appropriate to one stage may not be right for another. For example, a person who runs a one-man business does not need to worry about delegating – but when he / she has a dozen employees, delegating becomes more important than doing.

You should be thinking about managing long before you have anyone to manage. The starting point is your own strengths and weaknesses as an entrepreneur. Go back to the *Self-assessment* and *Training for Entrepreneurs* section in the first chapter, **READY**. Look again at your skills and training needs.

Consider whether a partner or key employee could supply some of the skills you are missing. Use the panel to identify critical areas in your business and those where a partner or key manager could make a difference. Could your business bear the financial impact of another salary? One that would make a critical difference to the speed at which your business develops? Could you reduce your own salary for a while to compensate?

CRITICAL BUSINESS AREAS

Which of these areas are most critical to the development of your business? Where would a partner or key manager make the most difference? Rank them 1, 2, 3, etc.
- Marketing
- Sales
- Financial control
- Production
- Management

If you are to build a strong team, you need to become a good manager yourself. There are lots of books and courses available to help you here. You need to build skills in delegation, time management, coaching, appraisal and communications to name but a few. But one of the most important points to make is that successful managers show, in lots of little but important ways, that they care for their staff, that they trust them and that they are willing to allow them to use their initiative (and to make mistakes!).

Good managers listen, they are interested in people in and outside work, they share information and knowledge, they are open to new ideas, they are enthusiastic and have a sense of humour. Check your own management style by answering the questions in the panel.

STAFF RETENTION

It may seem strange to consider staff retention before you have even recruited your first employee but, as in many things, forward planning pays off.

Staff are a key success factor in any business. Managing staff has implications in every part of the business as very often your staff will be responsible for implementing all the bright ideas you come up with. They can make or break your ideas. And, properly encouraged, they can produce bright ideas of their own. Therefore, a lot of time and thought should be given not only to considering whom you want to recruit but also how to keep your staff happy and productive. To see why this is important, consider the costs of staff turnover:

- **Loss of capacity:** There's no one there to do the work, until you find a replacement
- **Loss of knowledge:** All that the person has learnt, before joining and in your business, is **gone**
- **Loss of experience:** All the experience the person had is gone
- **Loss of network:** All the contacts that the person had are gone – some other employer has these now (are they a competitor of yours?)
- **Loss of training:** All the training you gave the person is gone
- **Cost of recruitment:** You will have to spend time and money recruiting a replacement and may have to pay the new person more than the person who left
- **Cost of induction:** The new person will take a little while to settle in, during which time they are producing below expected output and a drain on the time of other staff
- **Cost of new training:** You may have to train the new person.

All this makes it worth minimising staff turnover.

WHICH LEGAL STRUCTURE?

When starting in business, you have a choice of four main types of business entity through which to conduct your enterprise. They are:

- Sole trader
- Partnership
- Limited liability company
- Co-operative.

Four things will decide which structure you choose:

- **The kind of business you are starting:** Some professional firms can only be formed as sole traders or partnerships

- **The expectations of those with whom you plan to do business:** Many business people expect to deal with limited companies and are wary of other forms of business entities as trading partners

- **Your attitude to risk:** In particular, to risking those of your assets that you are not planning to commit to the business. A limited liability company limits the risk of losing your capital if your enterprise is not successful

- **How you wish to organise your tax affairs:** Certain kinds of favourable tax treatment are only available to limited liability companies.

You are taking a risk in starting an enterprise. You are risking your money, time and reputation. You are entitled to protect those of your assets that you do not wish to commit. For this reason, you are strongly advised to form a limited liability company. However, because of the tax and other implications of doing so, you should take professional help and advice before making your decision.

Sole Trader

You automatically become a sole trader by starting up a business on your own. Setting up as a sole trader needs almost nothing by way of legal formality, apart from registering with the Registrar of Business Names at the Companies Registration Office (**www.cro.ie**) if they trade under a name that is not their own.

An advantage of being a sole trader is that apart from normal tax returns, which every taxable person must make, a sole trader is not required to make public any information about the business. The downside of being a sole trader is that you have no protection if your business fails. All your assets become available to pay off your creditors.

One of the most fruitful sources of ruin to men of the world is the recklessness or want of principle of partners, and it is one of the perils to which every man exposes himself who enters into business with another.
SIR R MALINS

Partnership

A partnership, essentially, is an agreement between two or more people to go into business together. It may be no more formal than a handshake or may run to a multi-page legal document. Whichever route you take, build the following points into your planning:

- In a partnership, each partner is liable for all the liabilities of the business. If the business fails, and your partner(s) abandon(s) you, you could be left to pay for everything out of your own pocket. Before entering a partnership, decide whether you trust your partner(s)-to-be with everything you own — because that's what you will be doing.

- If you write down nothing else, write down and have all the partners sign a partnership agreement setting out how the business is to be financed, how profits and losses are to be shared, and what will happen if one of the partners decides to leave.

These are important points. Failure to agree on them at an early stage can lead to difficulty later.

A limited liability company

A limited liability company is a legal entity separate from its shareholders. The shareholders are only liable, in the event of the business becoming unable to pay its debts, for any amount outstanding on their subscribed shareholdings.

Some limited companies are limited by guarantee – the guarantee being the amount that the members agree to pay in the event of the company going into liquidation. This form of company is more suitable for clubs and associations than for trading businesses.

The advantages of a limited company over a sole trader or partnership are:

- Limited liability status
- The possibility of obtaining credit more easily
- The only income taxable on the owners of the business is any salaries or dividends taken from the business
- Some State grants and tax incentives are only available to limited companies
- Scope for tax planning.

The disadvantages include:

- The cost of formation expenses
- The requirement for an annual audit (in some circumstances, this is not required for companies limited by shares)
- The public filing of information with the Companies Registration Office

- The need for accounts to comply with Companies Acts and accounting standards
- Business losses may not be set against personal income
- Possibility of further taxation on capital gains if appreciating assets are taken from the business.

A limited liability company may use "Limited" or "LTD" (or the Irish equivalents) in its name, unless it is a Designated Activity Company – one that has specific "Objects" in its Constitution, which limit the range of its lawful activities – in which case it uses "DAC".

EU regulations allow the formation of private limited companies with only one member and the *Companies Act, 2014* permits LTD companies to have only one director, although DACs still require two directors.

More information, as well as registration forms, are available for download from **www.cro.ie**.

A co-operative

A worker co-operative is where a team comes together to form and run a business according to a set of values that include self-help, self-responsibility, democracy, equality, equity and solidarity. The business is jointly owned and democratically controlled, unlike other more hierarchical business structures. Co-operative members believe in the ethical values of honesty, openness, social responsibility and caring for others.

The Co-operative Principles, which provide guidelines setting out how the business should conduct itself, are:

- **Voluntary and open membership:** Co-operatives do not permit gender, social, racial, political or religious discrimination and are open to all willing to accept the responsibilities of membership
- **Democratic member control:** Co-operatives are democratically controlled by their members, who actively participate in setting policies and in decision-making
- **Member economic participation:** Members contribute equitably to the capital of their business. Surpluses are used to develop the business, benefiting members in proportion to their transactions with the co-operative and supporting activities approved by the membership
- **Autonomy and independence:** In all contracts with external bodies, co-operatives ensure that members retain democratic control and their co- operative autonomy
- **Education, training and information:** Co- operatives provide education and training for their members and employees to ensure their effective contribution
- **Co-operation among co-operatives:** Co- operatives work

together through local, regional, national and international structures

- **Concern for community:** Co-operatives work for sustainable development through policies approved by their members.

Formation of co-operatives is by Model Rules. Co-operatives can be formed as limited companies.

Directors' responsibilities

If you are a director of a limited liability company, you take on responsibilities – and the enforcement regime for these is increasingly strict – including:

- Responsibilities given under the company's Constitution
- Responsibilities imposed by company law, which extend directors' fiduciary duties under common law.

The *Companies Act, 2014* codified the responsibilities of directors – setting out a "clear expression of what is required by directors" – and established significant fines and penalties (including jail sentences) for offences.

Directors owe a duty to exercise skill and diligence in their work, in line with their knowledge and experience, though they cannot be held responsible in law for errors of judgement. In certain circumstances, directors may become personally liable for the debts of a company – for example, where it can be shown that they are guilty of reckless or fraudulent trading, or where the company has failed to keep 'proper books of account'.

On a day-to-day basis, the Companies Acts impose requirements on directors for ensuring compliance in relation to returns of information – for example, an Annual Return each year following the AGM. Following many years of non-compliance (or, at best, lax compliance, even among sizeable companies), the Companies Registration Office, backed by the Director of Corporate Enforcement, is now taking a harsher view and imposing penalties and 'striking off' companies for late returns. The impact of this is that, where a company continues to trade after it has been struck off, the directors become personally liable for its debts.

In company secretarial work and your responsibilities as a director, take advice from your accountant.

BUSINESS NAMES

Choosing a business name

The name of a business is one of its most important assets, even though it does not appear in the balance sheet with the other assets. Choose the name of your business carefully.

The right name will be:

- Unique
- Easy to remember, pronounce and spell
- Informative
- Image-creating
- Available as a domain name.

If your business is going to trade as a limited liability company, there are some restrictions on the name you choose (see panel).

CHOOSING A COMPANY NAME

You may NOT use as a name for a limited company any name that:

- Is identical to the name of an existing company
- Is offensive
- Implies State sponsorship
- Uses certain restricted words, such as "Bank", "Banker", or "Banking", "Society", "Co-op", "Co-operative" or "Insurance".

Even if your business is not going to trade as a limited company, there are still some rules to be followed. You still cannot use the name of an existing business, or one that will be confused with the name of an existing business. However, a partnership can use the same name as an existing partnership, provided the name consists only of the names of the partners. In general, follow the rules for companies above.

Note that you can now "reserve" a company name for 28 days (for a fee), before committing to registering it.

Registering a business name

If, trading as a limited company, you wish to trade under a name other than the company's registered name (for example as *West Cork Forest Advisory Services*, though the company is registered as *Frank Kelly Limited*), you must register the business name.

If you are trading in one of the other business structures, it is advisable to register the name of the business.

However, note that registration of a business name does not:

- Give protection against duplication of the name (since others may be entitled to use it, though you can prevent them from 'passing off' – pretending to be you)

- Imply that the name will prove acceptable as a company name (it may already be registered, or become registered later, as a company name)
- Authorise the use of the name, if its use could be prohibited for other reasons — for example, because the name proposed is the trade mark of another person.

Because of this last point, it is important to check whether someone else might have rights in the proposed name before spending money on stationery, signs etc. Check on the Companies Registration Office website (**www.cro.ie**) for registration forms and procedures.

On registration of your business name, you will be issued with a Certificate of Business Name – for August 2016, a "digitally certified" document (in PDF format) will be issued by the Companies Registration Office. This must be displayed prominently at the company's registered or principal office and in every branch or premises.

Domain names

A domain name identifies your business on the Internet. This is why it's important to have a name in the form **www.yourcompany.com** rather than **www.webhost.com/ ~yourcompanyname**. The latter is like putting "We're not a very important company" on your letterhead!

The suffix (.com or .ie) is determined by where your name is registered. Names registered with US agencies get a .com address. The reason there are so many of these (and why so many non-US websites have them) is that they are easy to get, with little formality beyond payment. The downside of this is that many names have already been acquired – some by people who plan to use them for their business, others by people who hope to sell them on to someone else at a profit (cyber-squatting). You can register a .com domain name at, for example, **www.godaddy.com** or **www.blacknight.ie**.

Irish domain names, distinguished by the .ie suffix, are registered through the IE Domain Registry (**www.iedr.ie**). To prevent cyber-squatting, IEDR requires proof that you have an entitlement to use the name you ask for – for example, it is the name of a limited company or registered business name that you own. Since IEDR also requires hosting information, it is often easier to let your ISP register your domain name.

Just like a company name, a domain name must be distinctive and memorable. Ideally, it should be your business name but it could be a brand name or some other more general descriptive name.

BANK ACCOUNTS

At least one bank account is essential for any business, however small. Don't be tempted to run your business through your own personal bank account 'until it gets off the ground'. That is a recipe for disaster. Open a separate bank account for your business as soon as you begin to trade.

OBJECTIVES

o Understand the steps involved in opening a business bank account

Opening a bank account

A limited company needs to pass a resolution of the Board of Directors to open a bank account. The steps are:

- Ask your bank manager for a bank mandate form; this authorises the bank to carry out the instructions of the directors regarding the operation of the account

- Decide what instructions you want to give the bank regarding who is authorised to sign cheques on behalf of the company, and how often you want to receive statements

- Hold a meeting of the directors of the company

- Propose the resolution at the meeting in the form required by the bank – see the mandate form for the wording – and have the resolution adopted by the directors

- Complete the mandate form, including sample signatures from each of the people authorised to sign cheques on behalf of the company

- Return the mandate form and sample signatures to your bank manager

- Give the bank manager a copy of your company's Constitution for the bank's files

- Show the original of the company's Certificate of Incorporation to your bank manager. A copy of this will be taken for the bank's files and on the copy will be marked the fact that the original has been seen by the manager. You should not give the bank manager the original Certificate of Incorporation without getting a receipt for the certificate and a date when you can return to collect it

- If you are trading under a registered business name, you will also need to show the bank manager the Certificate of Registration of Business Name for the company

- Have available some money to lodge to the new account

Depending on the bank and branch, it may take a few days or a few weeks to clear all the paperwork associated with opening your company's bank account. Allow for this in your planning.

TAXATION

OBJECTIVES

o Understand the system of taxation

o Understand the basics of individual taxes

Businesses in Ireland are subject to:

- **Income tax:** Sole traders and partnerships on their profits
- **Corporation tax:** Limited companies on their profits
- **Value added tax (VAT):** All businesses with turnover in excess of €75,000 (goods) or €37,500 (services)
- **PAYE / PRSI:** All businesses with employees (including owner / directors).

Registration for tax

It is your obligation to notify the Revenue Commissioners through your local tax office of the establishment of your business and to provide them with the information required to register your business for the relevant taxes.

You must complete one of two forms:

- Form TR1, if you are a sole trader or partnership
- Form TR2, if your business is a limited company.

Each of these forms gets you registered for all applicable taxes. They are available for download on the Revenue's website. Shortly after registration, you may receive a 'new business visit' from a Revenue official who will go through the requirements to ensure that you have proper systems in place.

CORPORATION TAX

To serve the community by fairly and efficiently collecting taxes and duties and implementing import and export controls.
REVENUE COMMISSIONERS' MISSION

There's nothing so hard to understand as the income tax.
ALBERT EINSTEIN

The trick is to stop thinking of it as "your" money.
ANONYMOUS UK REVENUE AUDITOR

Limited companies pay Corporation Tax. This tax is charged on the company's profits, which include both income and chargeable gains.

A company's income for tax purposes is calculated in accordance with Income Tax rules (see below). Chargeable gains are calculated in accordance with Capital Gains Tax rules. If an individual is trading through a company, any losses arising can only be offset against trading income of the company or against future or past profits, subject to certain restrictions – not against any other personal income earned.

Self-assessment

The self-assessment system applies to companies. Preliminary Tax is payable within six months of the end of the accounting period, which is generally the period for which the company makes up its accounts. To avoid penalties and interest charges, Preliminary Tax paid must be 90% of the final liability for the period. A company must submit a return (Form CT1) no later than nine months from the end of the accounting period to which the return relates. If the Preliminary Tax paid was insufficient, the balance of tax is payable within one month of the issue of the assessment by the Inspector of Taxes. There are also restrictions on the use the company can make of certain reliefs and allowances if the return is not submitted on time.

There are two rates of Corporation Tax:

- 12.5% on trading income
- 25% on non-trading income.

New companies carrying on a qualifying trade are entitled to tax relief on their profits for the first three years: where the company's total Corporation Tax liability is less than €40,000 for the year, relief is allowed for the amount of Employer's PRSI paid, subject to a limit of €5,000 per employee and €40,000 overall.

INCOME TAX

Income tax is payable by individuals on income earned in the tax year – that is, on annual profits or gains from an individual's trade, profession or vocation and on other income, such as investment income, rental income etc.

A tax assessment is usually based on actual income earned in the tax year – from 1 January to 31 December. It is up to the individual / business to decide the date to which the accounts are prepared, usually to the same date each year.

A self-employed person will be taxed under the Self-Assessment system.

Preliminary Tax is an estimate of the income tax payable for the year. It includes PRSI and USC, as well as income tax. The duty lies on the individual to calculate their own Preliminary Tax. If Preliminary Tax is not paid by the due date, or if the amount is too low, penalties and interest charges will apply. Failure to submit a tax return by the tax return filing date will result in a surcharge being added to the final tax bill.

Where a new business is set up, the surcharge will not be imposed if the return for the first year is made by the return filing date for the following year.

An explanatory booklet (IT10) on *A Guide to Self-Assessment* is available from the Revenue website (**www.revenue.ie**).

Calculating taxable profits

Taxable profits are calculated by deducting allowable business expenses from turnover. Turnover is the gross amount of income earned by a business before deducting any business expenses – the total amounts from sale of goods or provision of services. If a business is registered for VAT, the turnover figure should exclude VAT.

If a business makes a loss, it is either offset against other taxable income or carried forward against the future profits of the business.

Business expenses are normally referred to as revenue expenditure, which covers day-to-day running costs (exclusive of VAT, if the business is registered for VAT), including:

- Purchase of goods for resale
- Wages, rent, rates, repairs, lighting, heating etc.
- Running costs of vehicles or machinery used in the business
- Accountancy and audit fees
- Interest paid on any monies borrowed to finance business expenses / items
- Lease payments on vehicles or machinery used in the business.

Some expenses cannot be claimed as revenue expenditure, including:

- Any expense, not wholly and exclusively paid for the purposes of the trade or profession
- Any private or domestic expenditure
- Business entertainment expenditure – the provision of accommodation, food, drink or any other form of hospitality
- Expenditure of a capital nature.

For expenditure relating to both business and private use, only that part relating to the business will be allowed.

A deduction for the running expenses of a vehicle used for business purposes can also be claimed. To calculate the split of capital allowances (wear and tear) and running expenses, total mileage for the year and the total number of miles travelled for business purposes must be recorded. Journeys between home and a regular place of work are treated as private and not business mileage.

Expenditure is regarded as 'capital' if it has been spent on acquiring or altering assets that are of lasting use in the business – for example, the purchase or alteration of business premises. Capital expenditure cannot be deducted in arriving at the taxable profit. However, capital allowances may be claimed on capital expenditure incurred on items such as office equipment, business plant and machinery, taking account of wear and tear on them.

To arrive at the correct taxable income, the net profit should be calculated and any allowances and relief entitlements should be deducted.

Sub-contractors

Sub-contractors in the construction, forestry or meat-processing industries will have tax deducted at 35% (sometimes 20% or

0%, depending on the subcontractor's compliance record with Revenue) on all payments to them by principal contractors unless they have a certificate of authorisation (C2).

The decision as to whether a person is an employee or sub-contractor is matter of fact determined by guidelines set out in an explanatory guide for sub-contractors (IT64), which is available on the Revenue's website.

When starting a job as a sub-contractor, you must produce your C2 and sign a Form RCT1, which the principal contractor keeps. All payments to you then will be gross. Otherwise, at the end of the job, the principal contractor will issue you with a Form RCTDC, a deduction certificate, which shows how much tax has been deducted.

Whether you are paid gross, or with tax deducted, you are still liable to complete tax returns under the Self-Assessment system and pay any balance of tax due.

You can apply for a C2 at your local tax office.

PAYE / PRSI

The Pay As You Earn (PAYE) system operates on the basis that an employer deducts tax at a specified rate from an employee's pay. The system is designed so that, as far as is possible, the correct amount of tax is deducted from an employee's pay to meet his / her tax liability for the year. To achieve this, PAYE is normally computed on a cumulative basis, from the beginning of the tax year to the date on which a payment is being made.

In certain situations, it is not appropriate to operate PAYE on a cumulative basis and, therefore, tax is deducted on a "Week 1" basis.

In addition to deducting PAYE, employers are also obliged to deduct Pay Related Social Insurance (PRSI) from employees on behalf of the Department of Social Protection. The employee's PRSI contribution is made up of:

- Social Insurance, which varies according to the earnings of the employee and the benefits for which the person is insured
- Health Levy
- National Training Fund Levy.

The "tax credit" system operates as follows:

- An employee pays tax at the standard rate (20%) on all his / her taxable earnings for a pay period up to the standard rate cut-off point for that period
- He / she pays tax at the higher rate (41%) on all earnings for the pay period above this point
- The total of the tax due by the employee for the pay period is reduced by tax credits due to the employee in respect of the pay period.

The amounts of the standard rate cut-off point and tax credits due to the employee are determined by the tax office and advised on a Certificate of Tax Credits and Standard Rate Cut-Off Point issued to the employee.

Employers' PAYE / PRSI

When starting in business, you must register as an employer for PAYE / PRSI if you pay:

- €8 per week (€36 a month), or more, to an employee who has only one employment
- €2 per week (€9 a month), or more, to an employee who has more than one employment.

A company must register as an employer and operate PAYE / PRSI on the pay of directors even if there are no other employees.

It is important to distinguish whether a payment, benefit, expense etc. should be regarded as "pay" and taxed under the PAYE system. There are particular areas of benefits / perks (car, medical insurance, etc.) that have different tax implications.

Expenses incurred by employees while carrying out the duties of the job and for which receipts can be produced are not generally regarded as pay.

Registration as an employer

To register for PAYE / PRSI, employers must complete form TR1 (sole trader or partnership) or TR2 (limited company). You will receive confirmation of your registration as an employer, including a registered number for PAYE purposes and detailed information regarding the operation of PAYE / PRSI.

If you become an employer and fail to register for PAYE / PRSI purposes, the Revenue Commissioners will compulsorily register you. You will have to pay the PAYE and PRSI due – if you pay late, penalties and interest charges arise from the date on which your payment should have been made.

Payments and returns

PAYE and PRSI payments must be paid to the Collector-General within 14 days from the end of the income tax month during which the deductions were made.

A form P30 Bank Giro / Payslip is issued to the employer each month on which the figures for total tax and total PRSI contributions should be entered together with the gross total which will equal the amount of the payment. The form P30 should be returned marked "Nil" if there is no PAYE / PRSI liability for a particular month.

Employers can arrange to pay PAYE / PRSI through a direct debit scheme and make an annual return / declaration of liability.

At the end of the tax year, the employer must complete end-of-year forms P35, P35L and P35 / T sent by the Collector-General. These forms must be returned by the due date.

Employers must also issue a Form P60 to each employee who was in employment at 31 December. This form shows total pay, tax and PRSI contributions for the year ended 31 December.

VALUE ADDED TAX

Value Added Tax (VAT) is a consumer tax collected by VAT-registered traders on their supplies of taxable goods and services in the course of business and by Customs & Excise on imports from outside the EU. Each registered trader pays VAT on goods and services acquired for the business and charges VAT on goods and services supplied by the business. The amount by which VAT charged exceeds VAT paid must be paid to the Collector-General.

If the amount of VAT paid exceeds the VAT charged, the Collector-General will pay over the excess to the trader. This ensures that VAT is paid by the ultimate customer and not by the business.

Taxable persons

A taxable person for VAT purposes is an individual (other than an employee), a partnership or company that supplies taxable goods and services in the course of or in the furtherance of the business.

Taxable persons are obliged to register for VAT where the amount of their annual turnover (the amount of receipts excluding VAT) exceeds or is likely to exceed €75,000 – goods or €37,500 – services.

Traders whose turnover is below these limits are not generally obliged to register for VAT but may do so if they wish.

The main current rates of VAT are:

- **23% (standard rate):** All goods and services that are not exempt or are taxable at the zero or reduced rates
- **13.5%:** Certain fuels (coal and domestic gas), building and building services, newspapers, certain other goods and services
- **9%:** Tourism and related activities
- **4.8%:** Livestock, live greyhounds and the hire of horses
- **Zero:** Exports, certain food and drink (bread and milk), oral medicine, books excluding newspapers, brochures
- **Exempt:** Financial, medical and educational activities.

Within the EU, VAT is charged (if applicable) on online transactions in the country in which the transactions originate – except for electronic services, when VAT is based on the customer's location. However, if your sales to other EU countries exceed certain limits, you may need to register for VAT in those countries. This area is still developing – check with your accountant / tax office.

Registration

To register for VAT, complete form TR1 (TR2 for a limited company).

Cash (money received) basis of accounting

Any registered person whose annual turnover is less than €2 million, and 90% of whose customers are non-VAT registered, may account for VAT on receipt of payment (money received) rather than on the issue of an invoice. This gives a significant cashflow benefit. Applications to use the cash basis of accounting should be made to your local tax office, after discussing the matter with your accountant.

Returns

When you register for VAT, you must complete a VAT3 form and return it to the Collector-General before the 19th day following the end of each two-monthly VAT period giving details of:

- VAT charged by you for the period
- VAT paid by you for the period
- VAT due to Revenue or repayable to you
- Goods supplied to / received from other EU member states.

You are required to make a VAT return even if you do not owe any VAT for the period.

An annual return of trading details is also required.

VAT may be paid through the Revenue's direct debit scheme. Any excess VAT will be repaid automatically by electronic transmission to your nominated bank or building society.

GENERAL

Record-keeping

The Revenue Commissioners have certain requirements regarding record-keeping and accounts (see *Accounting*), which you must comply with.

Returns

For each of the taxes, you are required to supply the Revenue Commissioners with specific information on or by specific dates. These are called "returns" and there are severe penalties for late submission or not submitting returns at all.

Information and assistance

Comprehensive guides to all aspects of business taxation, including a *Starting in Business* guide, may be obtained from any tax office or the Revenue's website (**www.revenue.ie**). Your accountant will also provide advice.

Revenue audits

A Revenue audit is a cross-check of the information and figures shown in tax returns against those shown in a business's records, covering:

- Income Tax, Corporation Tax or Capital Gains Tax and / or
- The returns submitted for VAT, PAYE / PRSI or Relevant Contacts Tax (RCT).

The Revenue Commissioners select businesses for audit by:
- Screening tax returns
- Carrying out projects on particular business sectors.

Generally, 14 days' advance notice in writing is given, stating the name of the person who will carry out the audit, the date and time of the audit and the year(s), accounting period(s) or VAT period(s) which are to be audited.

The auditor will examine a business' books and records to verify that the figures have been correctly calculated and that the tax returns and / or declarations for the different taxes are correct. If adjustments are required, the auditor will quantify these, discuss them with you / the appropriate person, seek agreement to the total settlement figure and issue written notification. Interest will be charged at 15% on tax underpaid where a taxpayer makes an incomplete or incorrect return and publication of an audit settlement may occur.

An explanatory booklet, *Revenue Audit – Guide for Small Business* is available from any tax office.

Taxpayers' Charter

It's not all one way, however. The Revenue Commissioners have issued a *Taxpayers' Charter*, which sets out your rights as a taxpayer.

Tax clearance

Generally, public sector contracts with or grant offers from State agencies (including the Local Enterprise Offices and Enterprise Ireland) are conditional on tax clearance.

If you receive grants of €10,000 or more, you must submit with your claim a Tax Clearance Certificate from the Revenue Commissioners confirming that your tax affairs are in order.

Form TC1 should be completed when applying to the Revenue Commissioners for a Tax Clearance Certificate. You will be given a TC1 application form by the agency or LEO.

Tax clearance will also be required in respect of each contractor, where sub-contractors are employed on a construction project.

Increasingly, like all Revenue interaction, the tax clearance system is moving online, reducing the amount of paperwork needed for compliance.

Revenue Online Services

The Revenue Commissioners are increasingly moving online. Not only are all forms and publications available on their website but Revenue Online Services (**www.ros.ie**) allows registered users to:

- View current employer taxes position online
- File and pay certain forms and returns online.

Talk to an accountant

Because tax regulations are becoming increasingly complicated, it is worth talking to an accountant about your specific situation and needs.

ACCOUNTING

Accounting – anything to do with financial matters – is the part of being in business that most small business owners like least. So they often neglect it, saying that it is more important to be "out there selling". Or they hand over responsibility for it to someone else – and forget about it. But you wouldn't do that with any other part of your business. You wouldn't hand over responsibility for marketing, for product development or for recruiting staff to anyone else. Why do it for something as critical to your business as accounting?

Accounting consists of three steps:
- Recording transactions
- Analysing them so that they provide information
- Interpreting them so that they are useful for decision-making.

Recording transactions

Let's start with a very simple paper-based system.

First, identify what transactions you need to record. Most businesses have:
- Purchases on credit
- Sales for credit
- Receipts – cash into the bank account
- Payments – cash out of the bank account
- Petty cash.

Let's start with these. For each transaction, you need to record:
- The date
- The type of transaction
- The other person involved
- The amount involved.

If you use a separate page for each type of transaction, you do not need to record the type of transaction – the page it is recorded on will tell you what type it is.

So you now have five pages for each of the transaction types with a limited amount of information recorded on each – the next chapter, **GO!**, shows examples of each of these.

Analysing transactions

Next, begin to analyse the transactions to provide information.

Take purchases on credit. You might analyse the transactions under the following headings:
- **Fixed assets:** Items not for resale
- **Stock:** Items for resale

OBJECTIVES

o Understand the basics of book-keeping

o Appreciate the need for records and regular accounts

A Tradesman's Books, like a Christian's Conscience, should always be kept clean and clear; and he that is not careful of both will give but a sad account of himself either to God or Man.
DANIEL DEFOE (1660-1731)

- **Overheads:** Expenses incurred in running the business (analyse these further into categories – Staff, Production, Premises, Transport, Sales and promotion, General expenses and Finance – and further subdivide if necessary to show the detail you need)
- **Miscellaneous / Sundry:** Items for which you can find no other obvious category or which happen so seldom that it's not worth setting up a separate analysis of them.

Sales on credit might be analysed by product / service type.

Cash into the bank account might be analysed by source, one of which will be debtors paying for goods / services bought earlier on credit. Other sources will include cash from cash sales (which should tie up on a daily basis), loans to the business, VAT and miscellaneous items.

Cash out of the bank account might be analysed by destination, one of which will be creditors from whom you bought goods / services on credit earlier. You might also have bought goods and services and paid by cheque, so you need to analyse these. In addition, you need to include overheads, using the categories above.

Small items of expenditure are recorded as petty cash expenses.

Value Added Tax

If your business is registered for it, recording VAT is the next step.

With certain exceptions (see the previous section, *Taxation*), VAT paid on purchases is recoverable, while you must account to the Revenue Commissioners for VAT you charge on sales. This means that, if the amount you pay for purchases includes VAT, you can reduce the cost to your business by the VAT amount. Similarly, you must deduct VAT from your sales before accounting for them in your business.

The "books"

The next chapter, **GO!**, shows the very basic "books" that you must keep.

Of course, you don't need to buy expensive accounting analysis books. Ordinary paper with ruled columns will do perfectly well to start with. Keep your sheets in a folder, with dividers for each type of page.

Use an extra column – perhaps one right in at the margin – to write the number of the transactions. Keep a sequence going from the day you start. And write the transaction number onto the receipt or invoice. File all the receipts and invoices away safely in transaction number order. Then, if there are ever any queries, you will be able to find the answers quickly and easily.

Bank balance book

Your bank balance is one of the most important pieces of information in your business. You need to know what it is on a daily basis. Since you have all the information you need to calculate it yourself, keep a Bank Balance Book. This is a simple ledger book (you'll find cheap versions in any stationery shop), with columns for:

- Date
- Transaction details
- Cash into the bank account
- Cash out of the bank account
- Balance.

An example of a bank balance book appears in the next chapter, **GO!**.

Record every transaction that goes through your bank account in this book, and you will always know what your balance is. Get into the habit of checking the balance before you write cheques (even if they are essential) and you will avoid unpleasant surprises. If your bank balance book shows that writing a particular cheque will make your account overdrawn and you have no permission to do so, you have two choices:

- **Don't write the cheque:** Strictly, it's against the law to write a cheque when there isn't enough money in your account to meet it
- **Get permission:** However bad the news, it's always better to break it to your bank manager in advance than after the event, when he is in trouble with his or her bosses over your unauthorised overdraft.

Yes, you are duplicating some of the information on your "Cash into the bank account" and "Cash out of the bank account" pages but your bank balance book can be written in summary form ("Cheque" will do under "Transaction details") to save time.

Transactions that originate with the bank (bank charges, interest and fees) should always be notified to you before they are charged to your account. As soon as you receive details of these amounts from your bank, write them into your bank balance book. Then you will be able to sleep easy at night, without worrying that the bank manager might call querying an unauthorised overdrawn situation.

Get into the habit of checking your bank statements when they arrive each month. Check to see that:

- All lodgements have been made
- All cheques have been cashed – you should deduct any cheques that you have written but which have not yet been cashed from the balance shown on the bank statement

- No charges or fees have been charged to your account without your knowledge.

If you find anything that you do not understand, however small the amount, check with your bank immediately.

"Still due" file

In addition to your bank balance, you also need to know who owes you money and how much. A simple way of doing this is to set up a "Still due" file – a folder into which you place a copy of every invoice you send out for sales on credit. As you get paid, take out the relevant invoice and tear it up. Adding up all the invoices in the file tells you how much you are owed. And the thickness of the file provides a quick visual check of the effectiveness of your credit control procedures (see below).

"Still to be paid" file

Another piece of essential information is the amount of money you owe – particularly to suppliers, who may stop supplying you if they don't get paid on time.

Open a file, into which you put a copy of every invoice you receive from your suppliers for goods or services you buy on credit from them. As you pay your suppliers, take out the relevant copy invoices and staple them to the cheque you are sending. Whatever is in your "Still to be paid" file at any point is the total of what you owe. In addition, your suppliers know exactly which invoices you are paying, since you have sent them a copy. Management information in two businesses, no less!

An information system

You can begin to combine, adapt and expand the "books" and files above to provide you with an information system, following your accountant's advice.

For example, if you have very few transactions, you might put all the "books" onto a single sheet of paper that you use to record all transactions for a day or week, whatever period is appropriate. Instead of filing away the receipts and invoices, staple them onto the sheet. In this way, the sheet becomes your "books" and provides you with an immediate overview of what's going on in your business.

As you become more familiar with the financial side of your business, you will identify figures that help you understand what is happening – sales each day / week / month, for example. Organise a system to extract and report these regularly.

Interpreting the figures

The next step is interpretation. Most of this is commonsense:
- If your bank balance is always overdrawn, you are spending

more than you are bringing in – and you will need to schedule (yet) another meeting with your bank manager

- If your purchases are high, and sales are low, stocks will begin to build up – and worse, you may not be able to sell the stock because it might be perishable, go out of fashion or become damaged
- If your overheads are high, you may be spending money on unnecessary items, like fancy office stationery and equipment, instead of on more productive items.

Talk to an accountant about the kind of information you need to manage your business and make sure that your system of recording and analysis provides it for you. And, of course, extracting the figures is only the starting point – you also need to do something about them.

Regular accounts

Every business effectively is required to prepare formal accounts once a year – some because they are limited companies and are required to do so by law, others because the tax authorities will need them to determine how much tax the business should be paying. But annual accounts are not much help in running and managing a business because:

- **They are too infrequent:** A year is a long time not to know what is happening in your business
- **They are prepared to a different format:** One that often is not helpful for decision-making.

So you need to consider preparing more regular accounts. Monthly accounts may be too much of a burden on your time and may not repay you with enough useful information but quarterly accounts are essential.

In preparing accounts, all you are doing is summarising the information you have recorded and analysed – the analysis helps you with the summary. You don't need anything fancy. A simple profit and loss account to tie in with your financial projections will do. Talk to your accountant, if you need help.

Spreadsheets

If you are a computer user, you will have noted that the "books" are ideal for conversion to spreadsheets. Simply replicate the format on your spreadsheet and use its functionality to provide totals, summaries, etc.

But, if you decide to go the spreadsheet route, take some simple precautions:

- **Include a date / time on every printout:** So that you can determine which version you are looking at
- **Make back-up copies of everything:** You do not want to have

to recreate your files from scratch at the end of the year or when the taxman comes calling

- **Consider locking cells:** To prevent them being overwritten by accident.

Accounting software

There are lots of accounting software packages that will do all this work for you – except the inputting of data, of course.

Some are very expensive and more suitable for larger businesses. But there are others – Big Red Cloud (**www.bigredcloudcom**), Xero (**www.xero.com**), Sage (**www.sage.ie**), Sort My Books **www.sortmybooks.com**) and Surf Accounts (**www.surfaccounts.com**) – that are suitable for small businesses and, because they are Internet-based, they are accessible from anywhere you have an Internet connection.

A computerised accounting system provides information literally at your fingertips when you need it (if you have kept your inputting up-to-date!). Talk to your accountant before spending any money, to make sure you choose the right system for your needs.

Credit control

Your "still due" file is the second element in your credit control procedures – the first is sending out accurate invoices on time. If you do not send out accurate invoices, customers will complain and delay paying you. Equally, if you do not bother to invoice customers as soon as a job is done, it suggests that you are not in a great hurry to get paid – and customers again will delay paying you.

Build a simple credit control system like this:
- Always invoice as soon as a job is done – don't wait for the month-end
- Make sure the invoice clearly states the date on which it is due to be paid
- File invoices in your "Still due" file in the order in which they are due to be paid, so that you can see at a glance which invoices are overdue
- Check your "Still due" file every week for overdue invoices. Telephone the customer to ask when you can expect a cheque. Get the name of the person who you are speaking to and ask for them the next time you phone
- After three or four phone calls, write. Say that you will have to put the account into the hands of your solicitors and / or cut off supplies. But only threaten to cut off supplies when you really mean it!

Some customers only pay when they receive a "Statement of Account", a listing of all invoices due which is usually sent to them at the end of each month. Find out which customers need this and make sure you send them a statement on time.

Also find out your customers' paying habits. For example, some businesses pay all invoices received up to the 27th day of the month in the first week of the next month. In this case, make sure your invoices are in their hands by the 27th! Fax or email copies, with the originals following by post.

KEEPING BOOKS AND RECORDS FOR TAX PURPOSES

You must keep full and accurate records of your business sufficient to enable you to make a proper return of income for tax purposes. These records must be kept for six years. Failure to keep proper records or to keep them for the necessary six years, where you are chargeable to tax, is a Revenue offence, punishable by fines and / or imprisonment.

The records kept must include books of account in which all purchases and sales of goods and services and all amounts received and all amounts paid out are recorded in a manner that will clearly show the amounts involved and the matters to which they relate. All supporting records such as invoices, bank and building society statements, cheque stubs, receipts etc., should also be retained.

You need to be able to account for:

- Your business takings
- All items of expenditure incurred, such as purchases, rent, lighting, heating, telephone, insurance, motor expenses, repairs, wages, etc.
- Any money introduced into the business and its source
- Any cash withdrawn from the business or any cheques drawn on the business bank account, for your own or your family's private use (drawings)
- Amounts owed to you by customers, showing the total amount owed by each debtor
- Amounts owed by you to suppliers, showing the total amount you owe to each creditor
- Stocks and raw materials on hand.

You will need to submit the following with your Tax Return:

- A Trading Account showing details of goods sold during the period and the cost of those goods, the difference being the gross profit / loss for the period
- A Profit and Loss Account showing details of gross profit and the various expenses of the trade during the period, the difference being the net profit / loss for the period
- A Capital Account showing details of opening and closing capital, net profit / loss for the period, cash introduced and drawings (not required from a limited company)
- A Balance Sheet setting out details of the business' assets and liabilities at the end of the period.

INSURANCE

OBJECTIVES

o Understand the different types of insurance

o Assess your need for insurance

When you start in business, you need to consider both business and personal insurance.

Business insurance

The main kinds of business insurance are:

- **Fire:** To cover rebuilding costs, etc. following a fire
- **Burglary / theft:** To replace stolen or damaged assets
- **All risks:** Coverage against loss of assets, however caused
- **Public liability:** Coverage against claims by members of the public
- **Product liability:** Coverage against loss relating to defective or dangerous products
- **Employer's liability:** Coverage against claims from staff
- **Motor insurance:** Coverage against driving accidents.

Most insurance companies offer these (or some combination) in a single "Office" or "Business" policy, which is more cost-effective than separate policies for each.

Other areas for which you might consider the protection of insurance include:

- Legal fees protection
- Credit insurance
- Bad debt insurance
- Computer equipment and data
- Travel
- Goods in transit
- Patents
- Business interruption
- Cyber security – protection against malware / virus attacks.

Since insurance companies rate risks differently, it is worth talking to an insurance broker, whose job is to find you the widest coverage at the lowest price. Ask whether you can reduce the premiums by paying an excess (just like motor insurance). Ask also whether the premiums can be paid over the year rather than all at the start.

People-related insurance

If the business is dependent on yourself, or one or two key staff, it is also a good idea to take out "keyperson insurance" on these people. Then, if they die or are unable to work, the insurance company will pay a lump sum to the company to help overcome the difficulty.

You may also want to look at life assurance (to provide "death-in-service" benefits), critical illness, permanent health insurance or medical expenses insurance for your staff. Here cost, and whether staff value the insurance, will be major factors.

Your own insurance

What insurance you take out on yourself depends on the risk you are willing to take, your budget, your family situation and what personal insurance you already have in place.

Look at the key risks:

- **You could get sick and not be able to work:** You need insurance to provide a replacement income (permanent health insurance)

- **You could get sick or die and have no one to take over the running of the business for you:** You need a replacement income plus enough extra to pay someone else to run your business (permanent health / critical illness / life assurance).

Talk to a life assurance broker about coverage against these risks.

Talk to him / her also about pensions, which can be a tax-effective way of transferring cash from your business to yourself.

CALCULATE YOUR MONTHLY INSURANCE PREMIUMS

Business insurance:
- Fire
- Burglary / theft
- All risks
- Public liability
- Product liability
- Employer's liability
- Motor insurance

Personal insurance:
- Health
- Disability
- Life assurance
- Pension

TRADING LAWS

OBJECTIVES

o   Be aware of key trading legislation applicable to your business

The Single European Market removed "technical" barriers to trade and thus opened opportunities for Irish businesses to export into Europe on a scale not possible before.

EU Directives set out requirements for the manufacture of a wide and growing range of products. Compliance with these Directives is shown by the CE Marking, which is assessed by the National Standards Authority of Ireland (NSAI).

Food labelling

The labelling of foodstuffs, in order to give accurate information to consumers, has become very important and increasingly regulated. The *Guide to Food Law for Artisan / Small Food Producers Starting a New Business* is available for free download from the Food Safety Authority of Ireland (**www.fsai.ie**).

Food labelling regulations are enforced by both Environmental Health Officers and officers of the Director of Consumer Affairs, who can enter premises where food is kept, manufactured, sold or transported, take samples, inspect documentation and take copies and examine, test and inspect products.

Most businesses involved in food preparation will have to be registered with the local Health Service Executive and comply with the requirements of the Food Hygiene Regulations; the Environmental Health officer of your local Health Service Executive will be able to give you details.

Licenses and registration

Most businesses can be started immediately but, in some cases, a license or registration is required. Examples include:
- Public houses and off-licences
- Driving instructors
- Employment agencies
- Taxi drivers
- Providing credit services.

Other trading regulations

You should check with a solicitor to make sure that you are not breaking any regulations, that you are operating in line with best practices and that you are up-to-date on the latest requirements.

Don't learn the tricks of the trade. Learn the trade.
ANON

Websites / emails

EU law requires businesses to show on all websites, blogs and emails details of the business, including:

- Name (and trading name, if relevant)
- Address (not just a PO box)
- Email address
- Company registration number, place of registration and registered office
- Licensing information
- VAT registration number, if VAT-registered (even if not selling online).

If you are selling online, you must display prices that make clear whether VAT is included, as well as the cost of shipping.

As a general rule, content on a website must be cleared for copyright and must avoid defamation.

Strictly, terms of trade must comply with legislation in each country in which you do business, though this may be difficult since there are few standards internationally, especially in consumer protection. The best protection is to make your terms of trade fair and clear – the 'golden rule' is to be transparent by:

- Giving your physical address
- Making it easy for people to do business with you
- Showing the full price of items, including VAT and delivery
- Giving a contact point where people can complain.

Data protection

Data protection is an evolving area. The *EU Data Protection Directive* says that personal information must be:

- Obtained fairly and lawfully
- Used only for the original specified purpose
- Adequate, relevant and not excessive to purpose
- Accurate and up-to-date
- Accessible to the subject of the information
- Kept secure and destroyed after its purpose is completed.

The Electronic Commerce Act, 2000 introduced the EU's Electronic Signatures Directive into Irish law, which means that electronic signatures and contracts have the same force as their hand-written or typed equivalents.

The General Data Protection Regulation (GDPR) comes into force on 28 May 2018 across the EU. Its objective is to give citizens control of their personal data and extends the reach of EU data protection to foreign companies processing data of EU citizens. It harmonises EU data protection legislation, making it easier for businesses, but brings in stiff penalties for non-compliance – up to 4% of global turnover! One to watch!

PREMISES

OBJECTIVES

o Understand the importance of physical location

o Understand the benefits and drawbacks of working from home

o Be aware of legal and other requirements

In *Marketing*, we saw how important place is as part of the marketing mix (4 Ps). In the property business, they say that only three things matter: Location, location, location. For certain kinds of business – shops, hotels, restaurants – location can make or break the business. But in all cases, the right working environment is important.

Choosing the right location

If you are looking for your first office, consider a serviced office or co-working space that offers administrative support (for example, telephone answering, message taking, photocopying, reception, etc.) It will save you hiring admin staff and buying equipment until the workload justifies it. These facilities usually operate on a rolling monthly rental basis.

For workshops and factories, you need to check lay-out, logistics, transport, weight of machinery, health and safety regulations, environmental issues, availability of three-phase electricity, etc. Draw out your ideal space before looking for accommodation.

Picking the right location for a shop or restaurant needs lots of market research. Major retail chains like Marks & Spencer are known to spend months monitoring pedestrian traffic outside possible locations before coming to a decision. Be prepared to spend several days standing outside what you think might be a suitable premises to check:

- Traffic flow (vehicles and pedestrians)
- Types of customers in the area
- Their spending patterns in other premises close by
- The timing of any rushes
- What other traders in the area think about the location
- What development is proposed for the area that might have an effect (positive or negative) on your plans.

Buy or rent?

This depends largely on how much money you have. But first consider whether you are in the product / service business or in the property business. It's very easy to get involved – and get your business' cashflow involved – in improving a property you have bought, instead of getting on with making your business a success.

Leases for rented properties should be checked very carefully. They may not always include all the terms the letting agent told you about – and, by the same token, will probably include some clauses he or she didn't mention at all. Have the lease checked by a solicitor. And don't rush to sign anything until you have completed your business planning, made sure of your financing and know what you are signing.

Other issues

Wherever you locate, consider insurance premiums, compliance with food hygiene and health / safety regulations, planning permission (for signs, usage, extensions, etc.), lighting, heating, alarms, signs, locks, insurance, toilets, interior decor, fittings.

PREMISES CHECKLIST

How important is location for your business?

☐ Very ☐ Reasonably ☐ Not at all

What is your budget for premises?

- Purchase
- Rent (annual)
- Renovations
- Fixtures & fittings

How much space do you need?
How is this to be divided between administration, storage, sales, production and other uses?
Will your customers visit your premises?
Do those visitors need to be impressed?
Is parking an issue?
Will you need space for deliveries?
Have you planning permission?
If renting, are you and your solicitor happy with the lease, as regards:

- Period of the lease?
- Rent (+ other charges)?
- Your responsibilities?
- The landlord's responsibilities?
- Terms for renewal / termination?

WORKING FROM HOME

Working from home is the simplest, and often the cheapest, choice in relation to premises for your business. It suits certain kinds of business but does not suit others. Think about combining working from home with serviced offices, where you will have a professional telephone answering / message-taking service, a "business" address and access to meeting rooms for times when your customers want to come and talk to you.

Planning permission

The use of a private residence for business purposes is usually subject to planning permission. In most cases, local authorities will not require planning permission (or deny it, if it is applied for) where there is no impact on neighbouring properties. For example, a financial consultant who does his / her paperwork at home but meets clients on their own premises would expect little difficulty in relation to planning permission. But opening a garage to tune performance cars might bring complaints from your neighbours – and a refusal of planning permission.

Conditions for planning permission to work from home vary around the country. Check with your local authority's planning department before making any decision.

A dedicated workspace

If you work from home, you need to set aside a clearly-defined "workspace". In this area – and in this area only – you work. When you leave it, you are "at home". If you do not do this, you will never get a break from your business, and will burn out.

Make your workspace a "Do not disturb" zone. If you are to work properly, you must be able to put aside the distractions of home life (telephone calls, children, visitors, chores) while you are in your workspace (just as you would in a "proper" office).

But it's MY home!

Bear in mind that working from home becomes complicated when you have employees. It may suit you to get up late and work in your dressing-gown, but what example do you set for your staff? And what happens when you want a day off – do you have to leave home in order to get away from constant queries?

Other issues

Your insurers will need to be informed if you are working from home. If you have business visitors, you may need public liability cover. You are also responsible for health and safety (your own and any visitors') in your home office.

WORKING FROM HOME – ISSUES TO CONSIDER

How much space do you need and where is that space available in your home?

How will you separate home and work (think about telephone, use of computers, use of space, home duties, etc.)?

What does your family think?

What image do you want to present (meetings, telephone answering, address, etc.)?

What are the costs and cost savings (both time and money)?

Use of technology?

What happens when you are on holiday?

What about the children (holidays, after school, when sick, etc.)?

Can you switch off or will your home office become a constant distraction?

Do you need planning permission?

FINANCE

It is said that there are only three occasions when you must pay attention to the way in which your business is financed:

- At start-up
- When you need additional finance for expansion
- All the time in between.

At start-up, you need to raise as much finance as possible in order to ensure that your business has enough money to get going yet, perversely, this is the time when it is most difficult.

The need to raise additional finance to expand a business suggests a successful business, which should have little difficulty in attracting the necessary funding – though not always.

In between start-up and second-stage fund-raising, and all along the way, your business will have a financing need that must be met day-to-day and planned in advance.

Start-up finance

There are basically only two types of finance:

- **Equity:** Capital invested in the business, usually not repayable until the business closes down finally
- **Debt:** Capital lent to the business, usually repayable at a specified date.

There are also only two sources:

- Your own money
- Someone else's money.

OWNERS' EQUITY

If you are putting equity into the business (and you MUST – if you won't, who else will!), recognise that this investment will be at risk. Decide whether there are assets you want to keep in your personal name or which you are not prepared to put up as security or to mortgage. Identify these and then look at everything else you own:

- How easily could they be sold and what would they fetch?
- Are they mortgagable assets?
- Will they be acceptable as collateral?

Before you mortgage your family home, obtain professional advice. Consider what would happen to the family home and your family if the business fails.

It is important that you raise as much finance as you can from your own resources, since most financiers work on a "matching funds" basis – they will invest no more than you are investing. This may mean being creative and including as part of your investment some items that would have been available to the business on an informal basis anyway. For example, if you plan to start a software business, you probably have your own computer and peripherals and probably intended using these in the business until it could afford to buy newer (and faster) machines. Put a value on them and include them as part of your investment, which might now be made up of €3,000 cash and €5,000 equipment – which looks better than just €3,000 cash!

In addition, you may qualify for a tax refund on your own investment in your business, if you meet the conditions of the Start-up Refunds for Entrepreneurs (SURE) Scheme based on income tax you paid in your previous employment. Check with your accountant.

If you can raise all the money you need from your own resources, then you can count yourself lucky and move further on in this section. Everyone else, keep reading!

OUTSIDE EQUITY

Before you raise outside equity, you need to be prepared to allow other people to own part of your business. This sounds logical, but many entrepreneurs forget it and react badly when their investors begin to want some involvement in the business in return for their investment.

If you are looking for outside equity, there are three types to consider:
- **Seed capital:** Less than €250,000, for start-ups
- **Venture capital:** Between €250,000 and €1,000,000, for businesses at an early stage of development
- **Development capital:** €1,000,000+, for expansion.

Seed capital is the one you probably want. Unfortunately, it is also the hardest to get, although the recent success of Irish technology companies means that there is funding available, sometimes linked to incubation facilities.

Sources of equity
The first sources you should try are:
- **Family and friends:** Depending on your personal circumstances, this can be a fruitful source. But make sure they understand the risks involved and can afford to lose an investment. Put agreements in writing
- **Business contacts:** It's worth checking to see whether someone you know in business will help you get started with a small investment

- **Business angels:** Professional investors who may take an active role in managing the business as well as providing finance
- **Crowdfunding:** Raising small amounts of finance from lots of people, usually giving a gift or a sample product instead of equity. A number of websites – **Kickstarter.com** and **FundIt.ie** are the best known – provide a marketplace for crowdfunding.

Before you turn to the professionals – the venture capital funds – look at incubators and accelerators. Many of these offer programmes that provide training and a seed investment in return for a small percentage of your equity.

Also, if your business qualifies (check with your accountant), consider the Enterprise Incentive and Investment Scheme. You could raise up to €15 million in equity, from investors who get tax relief on their investment. As you might expect, there are rules to be complied with – your accountant is the best source of advice here.

The Irish Venture Capital Association (IVCA) represents the VC industry in Ireland. Its website (**www.ivca.ie**) provides a list of VC funds and their interests.

OWNERS' DEBT

This is not a major source of finance for start-ups, since other investors prefer to see the owners' investment in the form of equity (more permanent than loans). However, it may be appropriate to put some part of your investment in the business as a loan (and thus repayable). Take your accountant's advice here.

OTHER DEBT

Debt comes in a variety of forms, from a simple loan from a friend with few conditions attached, through overdrafts, term loans, long-term loans, mortgages, etc.

Debt finance available to start-ups includes:
- **Overdraft:** The simplest form of bank finance. Basically, this is no more than permission to have a negative balance on your bank account. However, overdrafts must be cleared (and stay cleared for at least 30 days during the year, though not necessarily consecutive days) on an annual basis and the overdraft is repayable on demand
- **Term loan:** A loan for a fixed period, usually at a variable rate. Repayments include interest and capital
- **Long-term loans:** Sometimes subsidised by Government or EU

schemes, these aim to provide businesses with capital for 7 to 10 years

- **Mortgages:** Loans to buy business property, secured on the property itself, with fixed or variable rate options
- **Leasing:** A way of acquiring the use of fixed assets (for example, plant and machinery, cars, office equipment) by paying a regular monthly or quarterly payment, which is usually allowable for tax purposes. At the end of the lease, depending on the terms, you may have the option to continue using the asset for a small continuing payment or to buy it outright from the lessor
- **Invoice discounting:** A facility linked directly to sales, which maximises the cash value of debtors. The bank will pay you, say, 80% of the face value of an invoice when it is issued. The balance, less charges and interest, will be paid to you when the invoice is paid. Useful for the company that is expanding and in danger of being choked for lack of cash
- **Peer-to-peer lending:** Here, you borrow money not from a bank but from other businesses that have surplus cash. You can either organise this through direct contact or through a website like LinkedFinance (**www.linkedfinance.com**), where businesses are carefully evaluated before being allowed to borrow.

When considering financing your business with debt, you must consider:
- Fixed or floating
- Long-term or short-term.

Fixed debt is a loan that is secured on a specific asset – for example, on premises. Floating debt is secured on assets that change regularly – for example, debtors.

"Secured" means that, in the event that the loan is not repaid, the lender can appoint a "receiver" to sell the asset on which the loan is secured in order to recover the amount due. Thus, giving security for a loan is not something to be done lightly.

Because you have to pay interest on debt, you should try to manage with as little as possible. However, few businesses get off the ground without putting some form of debt on the balance sheet. The issues are usually:
- What is the cheapest form of debt available?
- What is the right balance between debt and equity?
- How to reduce the amount of borrowing required?
- Will borrowing be backed by personal assets / personal guarantee?

It is a good idea to try to match the term of the loan to the type of asset that you are acquiring:

- To avoid constant renewing / restructuring problems
- To ensure that each loan is covered by the break-up value of the assets in case of disaster.

For example, a loan to buy premises should be a long-term loan, unless you can see clearly that you will have enough money within a short space of time to repay it. Taking out a short-term loan or overdraft to buy premises is a recipe for disaster. You will have to renegotiate it time and again – and, if your business runs into temporary difficulties, you run the risk of losing everything if the bank calls in the loan.

Short-term loans and overdrafts are more suited to funding stock or debtors because you should be able to repay the loan once you have sold the goods or got the money in. Short-term finance is also used to fund other forms of working capital and cashflow. It should always be repaid within a year – even if, at the end of the period, you still need to borrow more to fund future cashflow. If you have to borrow the same sum of money against the same asset for longer than a year at a time, you should be considering longer-term finance.

If disaster strikes and you have to repay a loan suddenly, it will be much easier to do so if the value of the assets it was used to fund is roughly equivalent to the value of the loan. Thus, for instance, you would hope to sell your premises for at least as much as you borrowed to buy them. Machinery may be more difficult, as the resale price is rarely comparable with the purchase price. For this reason, unless the equipment you need is very specialised, consider buying second-hand for your start-up (although this may lose you grant aid).

If you can, you should arrange your loans so that unrealisable (or slow to realise) assets are purchased out of your own equity, using borrowing only for realisable assets. If an asset is easily realisable, the bank is much more likely to accept it as security.

Sources of debt

Sources of debt you should try first include:
- **Family and friends:** Depending on your own circumstances, this can be a fruitful source. But make sure your family and / or friends understand the risks involved and can afford to lose their investment. Put any deal in writing, with professional advice on both sides
- **Business contacts:** It's worth looking to see whether someone you know in business will help you get started with a small investment. Peer-to-peer lending is where businesses with surplus funds lend to businesses in need of funding, usually on a short-term basis and through an online exchange
- **Banks:** The main source of start-up borrowing
- **Credit cards:** If you have a credit card with a high credit limit

(and a low balance!), this may provide a source of funding (though more expensive than most). However, once your business is up and running, a company credit card not only provides an additional credit line but can cut purchasing costs and simplify administration

- **Credit unions:** Willing to help members start businesses, especially co-operatives, although loans tend to be to the individual who then lends / invests the money in the business
- **Finance companies:** Sometimes more willing to lend than a bank, as long as they can secure the loan with assets or personal guarantees. Rarely cheaper than banks, but may sometimes be prepared to lend when banks refuse
- **Microfinance Ireland:** First-Step Microfinance provides loans of up to €25,000 to start up or expanding new businesses. First-Step receives funding from Enterprise Ireland through the EU Seed and Venture Capital Fund and the Social Finance Foundation and is the beneficiary of an SME Guarantee Facility created within the framework of the Competitiveness and Innovation Framework Programme (CIP) of the European Community.

When looking for finance, beware of "specialists" who claim that they can find you money at favourable rates of interest if only you pay an up-front fee. Don't pay anything until you have the money.

Often, if you only need a small amount of money, the best way to raise it is to approach a bank with which you have already built up some relationship, whether on a personal basis or in a business capacity. The larger borrower may feel it worthwhile to seek professional help to put together a more sophisticated fund-raising package. Your accountant is the best person to give you advice in this area and may have contacts that will ease your path.

INITIAL INVESTMENT

The rule for funding a new business is: "As little as possible, as cheaply as possible". Do not put money into the unnecessary. It is better to start your business from an attic without a loan than in a glossy, but unnecessary, high-profile office with heavy bank borrowings.

On the other hand, do adopt a realistic position on the amount of money that you need to get going. Your financing will have to be sufficient to carry the business for a reasonable period before it reaches some kind of balance, when money coming in equals money going out.

In addition to capital investment in plant, equipment and premises, your financing may have to supply most of the working capital until sales begin to generate sufficient income to give you an adequate cashflow.

Try this technique:

- **Close your eyes:** Pretend to be in your new business. Look around you. What do you see? Make a list – from carpets to lamps, from computers to phones, from equipment to signs, from stock to the van for deliveries. Make the list as long as possible

- **Put a value on each item:** How much would it cost to buy new? Could you buy it second-hand?

- **Look at the list again:** Mark off the items you already have (chair, telephone, desk, lamp)

- **Calculate the difference:** This is the initial investment you require to start your business

- **Take it a stage further:** You need to buy all the items you do not have at present, but do you need to buy them all at the beginning or could some wait a few weeks or even months? What could wait?

Use the Initial Investment panel on the next page to calculate and record what you need to start your business.

Then go back through the list and take out what is not absolutely necessary. Be hard – take out anything that you don't REALLY need. But don't cut back so far that you will be unable to get the business off the ground.

What you are doing is what an investor or banker who reads your business plan will be doing – challenging everything to make sure that you have done your homework. Do it yourself before it's done to you and you will find raising finance for your start-up much easier.

Next, you need to put your initial investment into a format suitable for your business plan by identifying:

- **Fixed assets:** Property, renovations, fixtures and fittings, transport, machines and equipment, computers, etc.

- **Current assets:** Stocks, debtors

- **Cash**

- **Start-up expenses:** Expenses paid before the business begins, promotion and opening costs, etc.

- **Margin for unforeseen costs:** There will always be something you have forgotten or that could not have been expected when you did your planning. Allow for it here.

CALCULATING YOUR INITIAL INVESTMENT

	Need?	How many?	Have now	Need to buy	Cost New €	Cost 2hand €	Total cost €	Timing of purchase				
								Now €	Month 1 €	Month 2 €	Month 3 €	Month 4-6 €
Office												
	Y / N											
	Y / N											
	Y / N											
	Y / N											
	Y / N											
Factory / / / Workshop												
	Y / N											
	Y / N											
	Y / N											
	Y / N											
	Y / N											
Shop												
	Y / N											
	Y / N											
	Y / N											
	Y / N											
	Y / N											
Transport												
	Y / N											
	Y / N											
Other												
	Y / N											
	Y / N											
	Y / N											
	Y / N											
	Y / N											
TOTAL												

INITIAL INVESTMENT: ANALYSIS FOR BUSINESS PLAN	
1. Fixed assets	**€**
Property	
Renovations	
Fixtures and fittings	
Transport	
Machines and equipment	
Computers	
Goodwill, security deposits	
Other	
Total fixed assets	
2. Current assets	
Stock of raw material	
Stock of finished goods	
Work in progress	
Debtors	
Other	
Total current assets	
3. Liquid assets	
Cash	
Bank	
Other	
Total liquid assets	
Margin for unforeseen costs	
Total investment	

Copy this panel into your Business Plan, page 152.

Sourcing your initial investment

Now that you know how much you need (and what for), you need to find appropriate sources of finance. Re-read this section. Then decide how you will raise the money you need. Complete the panel on the next page, showing your sources of funding. If you have some sources already agreed, indicate this in the panel.

INITIAL INVESTMENT: PROPOSED SOURCES OF FUNDING

Personal assets available			€
Fixed assets			
Car			
Additional personal mortgage			
Savings			
Deferred loans (family)			
Other			
Total personal assets			
Introduced as:			
➢ Equity			
➢ Loans			
External equity			
➢ Source?		Agreed?	
External debt	Term (years)	Agreed?	
➢ Long / medium-term		Y / N	
➢ Mortgage			
➢ Loan			
➢ Leasing			
➢ Other			
Total			
Short-term finance			
➢ Overdraft			
➢ Suppliers' credit			
➢ Payments received in advance			
➢ Other			
Total			
Subsidies / grants			
Agency ?			
Local Enterprise Office			
Area Partnership Company			
Other			
Total subsidies / grants			
Total available finance			

Copy this panel into your Business Plan, page 153.

CHECKLIST FOR INITIAL INVESTMENT

Can you support the required investment in fixed assets with quotations from suppliers?

How did you estimate your stock levels?

How did you estimate the value of your debtors?

Do you have sufficient cash to fund on-going operational costs until sales begin to realise cash?

Do you have sufficient cash, or assets that can be quickly turned into cash, to cope with disappointments, delays and unexpected expenses?

Personal expenses

Just because you are starting a business does not mean that the real world will go away. You and your family still need to be fed, to buy clothes, to pay for food, clothing, heating, bus fares, mortgages, etc. You need to allow for this. Complete the panel on this page to calculate your personal expenses. This is not a target – it is what you need. It must be factored into your operating budget and business plan.

CALCULATE YOUR PERSONAL EXPENSES

	Week €	Month €	Year €
Expenses			
Rent / mortgage			
Gas, water, ESB			
Food			
House expenses			
Clothing / footwear			
Telephone			
Insurance			
Study expenses			
Memberships			
TV licence			
Transport			
Loan repayments			
Holidays			
Replacing fridge, etc.			
Luxuries			
Other expenses 1			
Other expenses 2			
Sub-total (A)			
Deductions			
➢ Children's allowances			
➢ Government benefits			
➢ Rent / lease subsidies			
➢ Spouse / partner's income			
➢ Other income			
Subtotal (B)			
Outgoings (A less B)			
Allowance for tax			
Gross taxable income needed			

115

FINANCIAL PROJECTIONS

OBJECTIVES

o Understand the process of financial projections

o Be able to prepare an operating budget

Budgeting is the process of estimating costs in advance, in order to:

- Ensure adequate finance for the business to achieve what it has planned
- Provide a control mechanism over subsequent spending.

With the exception of "zero-based budgeting", most budgets begin with the previous year's actual figures and make assumptions about the future:

- Adding a percentage for inflation
- Adding new costs and activities
- Deleting old costs and activities.

However, as a start-up, you have no historical figures to work from. And you're unlikely to be able to predict the future! Luckily, that's not what budgeting / financial projections require. Instead, you need to 'project' – based on one of more assumptions, to work out what your sales and costs might be in the future.

You can budget in two directions (often it is helpful to do both and compare the results).

"Revenue down" budgeting starts by working out how many units of your product / service you expect to sell and at what price. This gives you total revenue. Then estimate what percentage of revenue is accounted for by the various costs – Cost of sales (50% perhaps), Salaries (25%), Overheads (20%), leaving a net profit margin of 5%. Be careful with this method, since it's all too easy to scale up your budget beyond the point where you have exceeded your capacity to produce.

"Cost up" budgeting starts from the cost of making the product. To this, you add a profit margin big enough to cover marketing expenses, salaries, overheads and a profit. Multiply the total of product cost and the margin by the number of units you expect to sell to get total revenue. The difficulty with this method is that your selling price is unrelated to the market. In fact, inefficiencies in production are disguised by this method – until your product reaches the marketplace, when they are cruelly exposed.

Target costing is where you identify the maximum price customers will pay for the product and manufacture within this. Usually, this means that you have to look very hard at quantity, suppliers, materials used, the use of technology and alternative sources.

In the operating budget, you forecast:

- **Turnover:** Total sales

Know when to spend,
And when to spare,
And you need not be busy,
And you'll never be bare.
JAMES KELLY

Spare no expense to make everything as economical as possible.
SAM GOLDWYN

You never lose money by making a profit.
ANON

- **Gross profit:** The difference between the turnover and its purchase cost
- **Overheads:** All the expenses incurred in order to keep the business going
- **Net profit:** The gross profit less the overheads.

In developing your operating budget, take into account the expenses you will incur to keep the business running and to provide you, as the entrepreneur, with an income (your personal expenses from the last section), as well as the cost of meeting repayments if you have borrowed money. If you have a good idea of the overheads involved, you can calculate what the turnover figure will need to be, using the formula:

$$\textbf{Turnover – Purchases = Gross profit}$$
$$\textbf{Gross profit – Overheads = Net profit.}$$

Work out what you expect to sell (turnover) and how you are going to achieve this target.

Bear in mind that, because you will have busy times and not so busy times, your turn-over will not remain constant throughout the year. Budget for peaks and troughs.

At the same time, look at the forecast in light of overheads. Test these again against the turnover forecast. For example, does the number of visits planned to customers agree with the mileage that you have included in the Transport and Travel expense category (see below)?

Gross profit is the difference between the total amount for sales (turnover excluding VAT) and the purchase cost of the goods you have sold.

This gross profit can also be expressed as a percentage of the turnover (excluding VAT). A gross profit percentage of 45% signifies that for every €100 of turnover, €55 is purchases and €45 is regarded as the gross profit of the business.

Overheads

This section looks at the expenses that you will have in running your business, including:
- Staff
- Production
- Premises
- IT
- Transport
- Selling and promotion
- General expenses
- Finance
- Depreciation.

Staff

These expenses are only incurred if you actually have employees working for you (full or part-time). In addition to wages / salaries, you may (depending on the contract of employment) have to include travelling expenses, work clothes or uniforms, study expenses for employees, and so on. Bonuses, employers' PRSI and other staff-related costs should be included here also.

Production overheads

If your business has a production unit, you will have costs that cannot be directly associated with items of production – heat, light and power, maintenance, etc. – that can be treated as overheads.

Premises

This covers all expenses that are directly connected with your premises:

- Rent of premises (bear in mind the need to have the rental agreement checked by your solicitor)
- Mortgage interest, if you own the property under a mortgage
- A percentage of your personal accommodation expenses, if you begin your business from your own house (rent or mortgage split between the part used for business and the total, in m²)
- Repairs and maintenance, depending on the condition of the premises and, if rented, the contract under which it is used
- Gas, water and electricity expenses (enquire about these at your local authority energy department)
- Business charges and taxes, including service charges (if levied by your local authority)
- Insurance – fire insurance is essential
- Cleaning expenses – cleaning consumables or the cost of hiring a cleaner
- Miscellaneous small items (for example, hand tools, kitchen equipment, etc.) that are not depreciated.

IT overheads

Nowadays, every business has some IT overhead – whether it's for broadband access, a website or computer and printer consumables. Estimate it here.

Transport and travel expenses

First, you should estimate all the journeys by public transport that you are likely to make for your business. For car expenses, estimate the distance that you will travel on behalf of the business. The mileage should be multiplied by the cost per km –

which should include insurance, road tax, maintenance, depreciation, etc. Use Revenue-approved rates to avoid tax issues (see *IT54 Employees' Subsistence Expenses* and *IT51 Employees' Motoring Expenses*, downloadable from the Revenue website, **www.revenue.ie**).

Selling and promotion

The costs you estimate for promotion should be based on *Marketing – Promotion*, earlier.

General expenses

This category looks very simple but, in fact, it is frequently underestimated. General expenses include:

- **Telephone and postage:** Note that, if you work from your own house and make use of your private telephone, only the business-related calls can be regarded as expenses for the business and not the line rental
- **Subscriptions and contributions:** For example, to employers' or small business representative organisations, professional and trade magazines, Chambers Ireland, etc.
- **Insurance premiums:** Excluding the premiums for private insurance
- **Administration and office expenses:** Everything that you need in order to be able to perform your bookkeeping and carry on your correspondence (business stationery, envelopes, computer supplies, filing system, etc.)
- **Accountancy expenses:** Even though you may not have an in-house accountant, a bookkeeper can easily charge you several hundred euro monthly for compiling VAT and PAYE / PRSI returns and preparing the year end accounts
- **Entertainment:** Business-related entertainment of customers or potential customers should be included here. Note that entertainment costs are not tax-deductible.

Finance costs

These costs cover not only the interest on the loans you have entered into but also the expenses that are associated with the loan, such as credit advice, assessment, solicitor's fees, costs of arranging credit, etc. Remember that the repayment of loans is not a business cost but must be made from net profit.

Depreciation

Depreciation expresses the annual reduction in value of your fixed assets. There are various methods of depreciation. Though your accountant will choose the best method for your accounts, you can use the "straight line" method for your operating budget. Under this method, all fixed assets are reduced each year by a fixed percentage. For example, a machine costs €10,000, and will last for five years, when its scrap value will be €500. The annual depreciation is calculated as: €10,000 – €500 = 9,500 / / / 5 = €1,900 per year. The depreciation term is not usually changed during the depreciation period. Commonly-used depreciation terms include:

- Buildings – 40 years
- Extensions / renovations – 10 years
- Machines – 5 or 7 years
- Cars – 3 or 5 years.

OPERATING BUDGET – ANALYSIS OF OVERHEADS			
	Year 1 €	Year 2 €	Year 3 €
Staff costs			
Gross staff salaries			
Employer's PRSI			
Bonuses, etc.			
Staff training costs			
Other staff costs			
Total staff costs			
Production overheads			
Use of auxiliary materials			
Maintenance			
Heat, light & power			
Rent / lease equipment			
Insurance equipment			
Other costs			
Total production costs			
Premises costs			
Rent			
Heat, light & power			
Insurance			
Cleaning			
Maintenance			
Other costs			
Deduct:			
Rent received			
Total premises costs			
IT costs			
Broadband			
Website			
Consumables			
Other costs			
Total IT costs			

	Year 1 €	Year 2 €	Year 3 €
Transport costs			
Maintenance and repairs			
Lease costs			
Fuel			
Insurance			
Road Tax			
Public transport			
Air fares			
Deduct:			
Private use			
Total transport costs			
Selling and promotion costs			
Advertising			
Packaging			
Promotion			
Trade fairs			
Commissions			
Other costs			
Total sales and promotion costs			
General expenses			
Telephone			
Postage			
Subscriptions			
Insurance			
Stationery			
Office expenses			
Accountancy fees			
Legal & other fees			
Other costs			
Total general expenses			
Finance costs			
Interest on loans / / overdraft			
Mortgage interest			
Charges / fees			
Other			
Total finance costs			
Depreciation			
Property			
Fixtures & fittings			
Total depreciation costs			
Total costs			

Copy to Business Plan, page 154.

OPERATING BUDGET – ESTIMATE OF SALES / GROSS PROFIT

Revenue by product	Year 1 €	Year 2 €	Year 3 €
Cash sales			
A			
B			
C			
D			
Credit sales			
A			
B			
C			
D			
Total sales			
Deduct			
Opening stock			
Purchases			
Less Closing stock			
Cost of goods sold			
Gross profit			
Gross profit percentage %			

Copy to Business Plan, page 154.

OPERATING BUDGET – PROFIT AND LOSS ACCOUNT

	Year 1 €	Year 2 €	Year 3 €
Sales			
Cost of Sales €			
Gross Profit			
Gross Profit %			
Overheads:			
Staff			
Production			
Premises			
IT			
Transport			
Selling & promotion			
General expenses			
Finance			
Depreciation			
Total overheads			
Net Profit / (Loss)			
Tax on profit / (loss)			
Profit retained in business			

OPERATING BUDGET – ASSUMPTIONS

What assumptions did you make in estimating these key figures for your operating budget?

- Sales
- Purchases
- Stocks
- Staff salaries
- Production overheads
- Premises costs
- IT costs
- Transport costs
- Selling and promotion costs
- General expenses
- Finance costs
- Depreciation

Copy these Assumptions into your business plan, page 154.

MINIMUM TURNOVER

To calculate the minimum turnover to meet all your business and personal expenses, the formula is:

Total expenses x 100 / Gross profit percentage = Minimum turnover.

Calculate your own minimum turnover.

CASHFLOW PLANNING

OBJECTIVES

o Understand the difference between profit and cashflow

o Be able to prepare cashflow projections

On paper you could be the richest person in the world and still not be able to pay the mortgage (or go for a pint!). That is because there is a clear distinction between cashflow and profits and between costs and expenditure.

You need to know when money is coming in, and when it is going out. Cash is the lifeblood of the business and should be monitored rigorously. More businesses fail because they run out of cash than from almost any other cause. Even profitable businesses can fail because of lack of cash! So always think CASH.

The main pitfalls in financing are:

• Underestimating the investment needed (the golden rule is to double your original estimate)

• Not including room to manoeuvre in your start-up budget

• Forgetting your own personal financial requirement (how much do you need to take out of the business for living expenses?)

• Not putting aside money to pay your taxes when they are due

• Underestimating the difficulties of getting paid (the average credit period in Ireland is around three months).

When you calculated your initial investment (see *Finance*), you analysed your initial investment on a time basis – some items were needed now, others could be postponed for a month or two, or even more. Cashflow planning is the same exercise applied across your entire business. It means looking at every item of income and expenditure in your budgets and estimating when it will impact the business in cash terms. Timing of cash in or out can be critical – as you will find when your first big cheque comes in late!

Initial investment

You know when the items included in your initial investment need to be acquired; now calculate when they need to be paid for. Pencil in the amounts under the heading "Outgoing / Initial investment" in the appropriate months in your cashflow projections.

Be careful of VAT. You must pay it when you buy things but, even if you are entitled to recover it, you will not get it back for some time (see *Taxation*). Your cashflow needs to be able to pay the full amount up-front.

Next, look at sources of finance that you have agreed (see *Finance*). When will these come in? Pencil the amounts into your

Happiness is a positive cashflow.

FRED ADLER, US venture capitalist

Take the cash and let the credit go.

EDWARD FITZGERALD

cashflow projection in the appropriate months under "Incoming / Sources of finance").

Operating budget

Look again at your operating budget:
- Which items of expenditure will occur every month? (Don't forget your own personal drawings)
- Are there any once-off payments such as legal fees, security deposit for rent, new phone lines, insurance, etc.?
- Any advance payments for suppliers, rent, etc.?

Check your diary. Does activity in a particular month mean extra expenditure for that month? (advertising, direct mail, networking, meeting with your mentor, holiday, travel, etc.). Fill in those extra expenses. If clients have paid you (or will pay you) in advance, put that in the appropriate month. Do you have any forward orders? When will the product or service be delivered and when will the customer pay? Fill in the amounts in the appropriate months.

Go back to your market research and marketing plan. Are there seasonal patterns? Will some of your promotional actions increase sales in particular months? What are your expectations of how sales will develop in the first few months? Try to estimate sales for each month. Write down how you came to that estimate and on which sources and assumptions you have based it. Fill in your sales estimates in the appropriate months.

Check your cost pricing and, more importantly, the costs directly related to the sales (variable costs). Most obvious ones are purchase of materials and travel. Fill in the variable costs, and keep the VAT separate again. Things to check include:
- Do you have to pay VAT (calculate incoming VAT minus outgoing VAT)?
- Can you claim VAT back?
- When must you pay taxes and how much?

CASHFLOW PROJECTIONS – YEAR 1

	M1 €	M2 €	M3 €	M4 €	M5 €	M6 €	M7 €	M8 €	M9 €	M10 €	M11 €	M12 €	Year 1 Total €
Opening balance													
Incoming													
Sources of finance													
Cash sales													
Debtors													
VAT refunds													
Other income													
Total income													
Outgoing													
Initial investment													
Cash purchases													
Creditors													
Overheads:													
➤ Staff													
➤ Production													
➤ Premises													
➤ IT													
➤ Transport													
➤ Selling / promo													
➤ Gen. expenses													
Finance costs													
Loan repayments													
Personal drawings													
Fixed assets													
VAT payable													
Other taxes													
Other expenses													
Total outgoings													
Net cashflow													
Closing balance													

Copy this to page 157.

STEADY

CASHFLOW PROJECTIONS – YEAR 2

	M1 €	M2 €	M3 €	M4 €	M5 €	M6 €	M7 €	M8 €	M9 €	M10 €	M11 €	M12 €	Year 2 Total €
Opening balance													
Incoming													
Sources of finance													
Cash sales													
Debtors													
VAT refunds													
Other income													
Total income													
Outgoing													
Initial investment													
Cash purchases													
Creditors													
Overheads:													
➢ Staff													
➢ Production													
➢ Premises													
➢ IT													
➢ Transport													
➢ Selling / promo													
➢ Gen. expenses													
Finance costs													
Loan repayments													
Personal drawings													
Fixed assets													
VAT payable													
Other taxes													
Other expenses													
Total outgoings													
Net cashflow													
Closing balance													

Copy this to page 158.

CASHFLOW PROJECTIONS – YEAR 3

	M1 €	M2 €	M3 €	M4 €	M5 €	M6 €	M7 €	M8 €	M9 €	M10 €	M11 €	M12 €	Year 3 Total €
Opening balance													
Incoming													
Sources of finance													
Cash sales													
Debtors													
VAT refunds													
Other income													
Total income													
Outgoing													
Initial investment													
Cash purchases													
Creditors													
Overheads:													
➤ Staff													
➤ Production													
➤ Premises													
➤ IT													
➤ Transport													
➤ Selling / promo													
➤ Gen. expenses													
Finance costs													
Loan repayments													
Personal drawings													
Fixed assets													
VAT payable													
Other taxes													
Other expenses													
Total outgoings													
Net cashflow													
Closing balance													

Copy this to page 159.

SOURCES OF ASSISTANCE

A wide range of State bodies are charged with assisting entrepreneurs and potential entrepreneurs to develop their businesses. The assistance they provide may be in the form of cash grants but increasingly includes advice, subsidies, training, workspace, etc.

Whatever form it takes, this assistance may be vital in providing the final piece of the jigsaw to get your business up and running, or it may provide just the push you need to get going. Sometimes, it may even be just the fact that someone else has confidence in you that makes it all come together.

Grant-aid, or other assistance, is a good thing. It can help your business to grow. Going through the application process, whether or not you are successful, will focus your planning. But don't let the need to meet grant-givers' criteria push your business where you don't want to go.

Too often, entrepreneurs start by asking "Where will I get a grant?". Grants are not the aim of the business – your work on developing a strategy a should tell you that.

Grants are an extra, which may help you do something that you couldn't otherwise have afforded. They come at the end of the financing process – not at the start of the planning process!

However, if grants – or better still, relevant training courses – are available, take advantage.

OBJECTIVES

o Understand the place of grants in financing your business

o Identify main sources of grant-aid and other assistance

o Understand grant-givers' criteria

STATE ASSISTANCE

Overall responsibility for enterprise lies with the Department of Business, Enterprise and Innovation, which is responsible for promoting competitiveness in the economy and for creating a favourable climate for the creation of self-sustaining employment.

It works to monitor and improve the environment for business by ensuring that the framework of law, regulation and Government policy promotes effective company performance and both public and business confidence.

It achieves this indirectly by creating an environment for enterprise and directly through the agencies it has established, which operate to stimulate industrial development at different levels:

- **Nationally:** Enterprise Ireland (**www.enterprise-ireland.com**)
- **Regionally:** Údarás na Gaeltachta (**www.udaras.ie**)
- **Locally:** Local Enterprise Offices (**www.localenterprise.ie**) and Local Development Companies (**www.ildn.ie**).

Small and medium-sized enterprises are defined as independent businesses (fewer than 25% of the shares held by one or more large companies), that have no more than 250 employees, and have either turnover less than €50 million or total assets net of depreciation less than €43 million.
EU definition of small and medium-sized enterprises (SMEs)

IDA Ireland and Enterprise Ireland both report to the Department of Jobs, Enterprise and Innovation and implement policy set by it. IDA Ireland focuses on inwards investment — bringing foreign multinationals into Ireland — while Enterprise Ireland is tasked with supporting indigenous (Irish) businesses.

There are also other State agencies whose role includes that of stimulating development, albeit in specified sectors.

Where do I start?

The first question that you must answer to decide where you should look for help relates to the employment potential of your new business.

If, within three years or so of start-up, you are likely still to employ under 10 people, you should make your way to the Local Enterprise Offices and / or the other local support agencies.

Once you can show that you are likely to employ more than 10 people within three years or so of start-up (and meet some other criteria, including demonstrating significant turnover with strong export potential), Enterprise Ireland (or Údarás na Gaeltachta, as appropriate) may classify your business as a "high potential start-up" and takes you under its wing.

Rural businesses or those established in disadvantaged areas may find that Local Development Companies can support their early development.

STATE AND SEMI-STATE AGENCIES

As mentioned earlier, there are a wide range of these agencies, covering a variety of roles and responsibilities and reporting to appropriate Government Departments. This workbook's companion book – *Starting a Business in Ireland*, 7th edition – provides more details.

PRIVATE SECTOR SUPPORT

Private sector supports for start-ups in Ireland include:
- Accelerators
- Accounting firms
- Consultants
- Incubators
- Professional bodies and trade associations

This workbook's companion book – *Starting a Business in Ireland*, 7th edition – provides more details, as does the website, **www.startingabusinessinireland.com**.

REDUCING RISK

This workbook sets out what is probably the best way of reducing the risk involved in your start-up – producing a well-thought-out business plan. Next, you need to quantify the risks. The panel helps you to do that. It shows you what is at risk (your personal investment and any borrowings), how long for, and other factors that help you assess the risk.

When you have completed this 'STEADY' chapter, come back fill in the panel below.

OBJECTIVES
o Be aware of risk in start-ups
o Be able to identify and reduce risk in your business

QUANTIFYING THE RISKS

	€
Personal investment	
Total borrowing	
Annual cashflow	
Period personal investment is at risk	
Period borrowing is at risk	
Security given	
Time commitment over risk period	
Expected profit over risk period	
Salary required over risk period	

Sensitivity analysis

This technique looks at how sensitive your business plan projections are to changes – in sales, in costs, in the environment generally. Ask yourself questions like these:

- What happens if sales do not take off until month 8, even though the business plan projects month 3? How likely is this?
- What happens if sales are half the level projected? How likely is this?
- What happens if … ? How likely is this?

Break-even analysis

Another useful analysis tool is "break-even", the sales volume at which your business begins to make profit. This happens when Sales less Variable Costs (those that vary directly with output) covers Fixed Costs (costs that remain fixed over a wide range of activity).

Use the panel on the next page to calculate the break-even point for your business. If your sales expectations fall below this level, you have some work to do!

First ask yourself: What is the worst that can happen? Then prepare to accept it. Then proceed to improve on the worst.
DALE CARNEGIE

If your project doesn't work, look for the part you didn't think was important.
ARTHUR BLOCH

BREAK-EVEN	
	€
Sales price per unit	
Variable Costs per unit	
Fixed Costs (total)	
Break-even volume:	
Fixed Costs (total)	
divided by	
Sales – Variable Costs per unit	
equals	
Number of Units	
Number of Units x Sales Price	
equals	
Break-even Sales value	

Other risks

The other risk is that things can just go wrong. You can be unlucky. Answer the questions in the 'At Risk' panel to see how at risk your business may be.

AT RISK?

What happens if:
- You get sick for a long period?
- Your spouse / partner gets sick?
- Your computer breaks down?
- Your machinery breaks down?
- Your transport breaks down?
- How dependent are you on specific suppliers?
- How dependent are you on specific customers?

Consider both the probability of the situation happening AND its likely impact.

Protection

When you have identified the risks to which you are (or may be) exposed:
- Reconsider your Business Plan and look at alternatives
- Review your insurance situation (personal and business) – see *Insurance* earlier in this chapter
- Review your dependency (if any) on specific suppliers
- Review your dependency (if any) on specific customers.

MENTORS

Loneliness and a sense of isolation are the two most common complaints among entrepreneurs (after the difficulty in getting anyone to finance their business!). That's why it is so important to have the support of your family when you run your own business. But sometimes you need more than support – you need someone who has been there, done that, someone who has experienced what you are going through. This is where a mentor can be helpful.

A mentor is an experienced businessperson who makes available their experience and expertise to small businesses, usually for very modest reward. Most mentors are "putting something back into the system". There are several mentor schemes available – including Enterprise Ireland and the Local Enterprise Offices. Sometimes your bank or accountant may be able to suggest a suitable mentor.

Why a mentor? Then, who?

The first question to ask yourself is what you want in a mentor.

WHAT DO YOU WANT IN A MENTOR?

A sounding-board for ideas?
Advice based on previous experience?
Hands-on assistance, perhaps in implementing something new in your business?
Market knowledge
Contacts, to open doors that might otherwise be closed?
Expertise / experience in specific areas: Marketing, sales, finance, production, legal?

Next, you need to build a profile for your ideal mentor. Then, when you apply to the relevant agency, you will have a head-start.

WHO DO YOU WANT AS A MENTOR?

Someone:
- Older than yourself?
- Younger than yourself?
- With entrepreneurial experience?
- With managerial experience?
- With specific expertise?
- With specific industry background?
- From your own personal or business network?
- A complete stranger?
- Who will become more than a mentor (a friend)?

Discover someone to help shoulder your misfortunes. Then you will never be alone ... neither fate, nor the crowd, so readily attacks two.
BALTASAR GRACIAN

133

When selecting a mentor, act as if you were interviewing for a vacancy in your business (you are – for a trusted adviser to yourself). Aim to meet about three potential mentors and prepare carefully (re-read *Recruiting Staff* again). Go through the skills / experience match carefully. You may not be able to judge how good the mentor is at his / her specialist area but you can judge the chemistry between the two of you. This will be important, especially if you are looking for a confidante rather than an expert to solve a specific problem.

Working with a mentor

Your mentor must keep totally confidential everything you say to him / her. If you don't trust them to keep your secrets, get rid of them.

By the same token, you must be totally honest with your mentor. You are wasting your time (and theirs) if you are not telling them the full picture – deliberately or otherwise – and you may get wrong advice as a result.

Structure the mentor / business relationship as follows:

- Express your expectations from the mentoring process. (Write them down.)
- Allow the mentor to express their expectations. (If you have selected carefully, there will be no surprises.)
- Agree on what the mentor will do and what they will not do. Confirm confidentiality.
- Decide on what information the mentor needs to be able to help you.

PROFESSIONAL ADVISERS

An entrepreneur has to be a master of all trades. But, as your business expands, you may need to hire a consultant or specialist to assist in implementing a project or dealing with a problem that you are unable to solve on your own.

Choose carefully – a good consultant can add immeasurably to your business, while a bad one could cost you a lot of money with nothing to show for it. Ignore qualifications – they are necessary but not the basis for choosing a consultant. Look instead for experience. A good consultant will refer you to his / her previous clients. Ask other entrepreneurs whose opinions you value for recommendations.

Areas in which you should seriously consider employing a consultant (depending on your own skills, of course) include computers, accounting, taxation and law.

Reasons for hiring an outside consultant might be:
- To save time
- To gain information, knowledge and expertise in a specific area
- To get an independent view or a second opinion.

Selecting the right adviser is difficult. Just as with a mentor, before deciding on taking on an adviser, you should formulate some selection criteria.

Things to consider are:
- The consultant's knowledge of your business area and your specific project / problem
- His / her experience as a consultant and entrepreneur
- His / her way of working (dedicated to you until the project is done / available as necessary?)
- Ethics / confidentiality (can you trust him / her?)
- Costs (how / when will you be billed?)
- Time-frame (can the work be done when you want?).

Develop a clear briefing of what you expect from the adviser and ask for several quotes before you decide which one you are going to deal with.

Accountants

For information or advice on accounting or taxation matters, you are advised to consult your accountant.

If you do not know an accountant, ask other entrepreneurs whose opinions you value for recommendations to their accountants or contact one of the following accounting bodies:
- Association of Chartered Certified Accountants

OBJECTIVES

○ Understand how to work with, and what to expect from, professional advisers

I don't want a lawyer who tells me what I can't do. I hire a lawyer to tell me how I can do what I want.
JP MORGAN

To spot the expert, pick the one who predicts the job will take the longest and cost the most.
MURPHY'S LAW, BOOK TWO

- Chartered Accountants Ireland.
- Institute of Certified Public Accountants in Ireland

Any of these bodies will be happy to put you in touch with one of their members close to where you live / work.

Most accountants will not charge you for a first meeting. Use this meeting to help you decide whether you want to engage the accountant or look further.

Solicitors

You need a solicitor to:
- Check out any lease, loan agreement or contract you may be asked to sign
- Advise you on relevant legislation
- Act as the final step in your credit control process
- Act for you if you are sued.

If you do not know a solicitor, ask other entrepreneurs whose opinions you value for recommendations to their lawyers or contact the Law Society for a recommendation.

YOUR BUSINESS PLAN

All the research into success and failure factors of small businesses show that one of the most important success factors is business planning – over 70% of failures are due to bad planning.

Planning becomes even more important as the business develops. Business planning should be an ongoing process. All major companies have a business plan that is updated regularly. The same should apply for a small company.

A business plan has many functions, which change as the business develops:

- It makes an idea measurable
- It gives a complete picture of a business
- It gives insight into all the aspects of the business
- It assesses the viability of an idea
- It helps people to familiarise themselves with all kinds of possible problems
- It is a communication tool for use with suppliers, clients, advisers, banks, funds, etc.
- It can be used as a reference point in history
- It is a planning tool for the future
- It is a teaching tool for the entrepreneur
- It provides a step-by-step approach towards reaching a decision
- It is a way of assessing an existing business
- It is a working manual for the entrepreneur
- It is a checklist for the entrepreneur, bank, funding agency, etc.

Which functions apply to your business plan? Tick them above.

As a business goes through various stages in its life, it has different needs (see panel). In each, the business plan plays a vital role.

OBJECTIVES

- o Understand the process of business planning
- o Combine work done on earlier sections of the guide into a business plan

A good business plan is nine parts implementation for every one part strategy.
TIM BERRY

He hath made good progress in a business that hath thought well of it before-hand.
THOMAS FULLER (1654-1734)

Think of these things: whence you came, where you are going, and to whom you must account.
BENJAMIN FRANKLIN

Sit down to write what you have thought and not to think about what you shall write.
WILLIAM COBBETT

Always keep in mind that your business plan tells your story to those reading it when you are not present.
ANON.

BUSINESS PLANNING IN THE DIFFERENT STAGES OF A BUSINESS' LIFE CYCLE

Existence and survival
Thinking it through
Ensure solid base
Check viability
Convince yourself, your spouse / partner and investors
Consolidation and control
Decide further direction
Ensure progress
Confidence
Financing growth / survival
Control and planning
Secure finance
Communication tool to employees, partners and investors
Expansion
Maximise potential
Secure finance of growth
Stagnation
Revitalise company
Assess viability
Convince investors
Selling off the company
Sales document
Maximise selling price
Set terms of agreement

Growth is the goal, profit is the measure, security is the result.
SIR OWEN GREEN, BTR

The discipline you impose on yourself by writing things down is the first step towards getting them done.
LEE IACOCCA

A three-sentence course on business management: You read a book from the beginning to the end. You run a business the opposite way. You start with the end, and then you do everything you must to achieve it.
HAROLD GENEEN

It is always wise to look ahead, but difficult to look further than you can see.
SIR WINSTON CHURCHILL

Writing a business plan before starting a business reduces the trial and error factor (which is a very costly process) and will prevent obvious mistakes. The more effort you put into the business plan, the more you will get out of the plan.

Writing a business plan

The type of business plan you are going to write depends on the audience you are writing the plan for. It might be for:

- Yourself
- Your partner / spouse
- Potential business partner
- Private investors
- Suppliers
- Banks
- Local Enterprise Offices
- Others.

A good business plan is:

- Practical
- Honest
- Consistent
- Based on research and facts
- Complete

- Realistic
- Gives a clear picture of the personality and the quality of the entrepreneur
- Turn-key.

Structuring your business plan

Your business plan must have a structure that is easily followed and understood by the person reading it. Use the structure set out in the panel and then work through the example layout.

BUSINESS PLAN – STRUCTURE

Executive Summary

Introduction and Background
- Background to the company

Project Outline
- Overview of what the business is proposing to do over the period of the business plan – sales increase, employment increase, turnover increase, profit level increase

Ownership, Management and Employment
- Founders / Management
- Employee levels

Market and Marketing Strategy
- Overview of the market
- Projected share of the market
- Target markets
- Main competitors
- Key competitive advantages
- Marketing strategy
- Distribution

Production
- Products
- Increased capacity required
- New capital expenditure required
- Efficiency levels
- Skills and numbers of staff required
- Training requirements
- Quality
- Raw material sources

Financial
- Summary of projected performance

Funding Proposal
- Funding requirements
- Proposed sources of funding

Detailed Projections
- Assumptions
- Profit and Loss account
- Cashflow
- Balance Sheet

Executive Summary

This is the first part of a business plan to read – and the last to be written. Here, in less than a page, you summarise the key points of your plan. It's easiest if you can put them in bullet point, like this:

This Business Plan:
- Explains how XYZ Company came to be
- Describes the products we intend to make
- Describes the market
- Shows how we will reach that market
- Costs the products
- Includes Operating Budgets and cashflow projections
- Sets out the funding you require (if any) – for example, "Requests grant aid of €xxk, based on equity already committed of €xxk and loans agreed of €xxk."

See page 144.

Introduction and Background

This is the start of your business plan. Here you set out the basic information that a reader will want to know about your business:

- The purpose of the plan
- Business name and contact details
- Whether it is in operation or has yet to start
- The business objective
- The product / service range.

See page 144.

Project outline

Here you can go into more detail about the business:
- A description of the business
- Trends in the industry
- Targets that you have set.

This gives the reader a sense of what you are setting out to achieve. See page 144.

Ownership, Management and Employment

You, the entrepreneur, are one of the critical success factors of the business. For this reason, the reader of your business plan will want to know about you. This is not a place for boasting – simply explain why you believe you are a good bet to make a success of the business, based on:

- Your education
- Your work experience
- Your other experience.

If you have business partners, they should also complete this section. If your start-up is big enough to have managers employed (or key staff whose presence or absence will be critical to the business), you should consider including them here too.

If several people are included in this section, it may be best to summarise each person's details here and include the full information in an Appendix.

Since most of the State agencies, the Local Enterprise Offices, etc. are focused on job creation, it makes sense to tell them about the extent to which your business will contribute to job creation. Even though the agencies cannot grant aid part-time jobs, include them in your calculations anyway. And, where you are sub-contracting manufacturing or other aspects of your business, (even though again these are not grant-aided) include them also as "downstream" employment.

See page 145.

Marketing and marketing strategy

A critical section that will be read carefully by any investor. Because readers are unlikely to be familiar with your market, you need to set the scene for them:

- An overview
- Key indicators
- Target groups / customers
- Competitors
- Your key competitive advantages
- Your marketing strategy
- Your distribution.

See page 146.

Production

Again, because your readers may have no experience of your market, you need to explain:

- Your product / service
- How it is made / delivered
- The experience you have with the process
- What equipment you need (this ties in with your financial projections later)
- How you will assure quality
- Where you will source supplies.

If there is too much detail, put it in an Appendix. See page 148.

Financial

Most readers of business plans not only have a financial background, they are preparing to invest in your business. Therefore, they pay special attention to your financial section.

Here, you set out your financial projections – profit and loss account, cashflow and balance sheets. Whatever your own background, you need to be sufficiently sure of your financial projections to be able to withstand severe questioning. No one will invest or lend you money if you appear to be incapable of controlling it.

See page 150.

Funding proposal

This is the important bit – from your point of view. Here you lay out your stall. You have already explained what the business does, the market, the product, the financial projections. Now you are saying "I need €xxk, made up as follows. I have €xxk of my own. I have tied down €xxk more from these sources. I need €xxk, please".

Again, you need to be very sure of your calculations here. If some figures are loose – you think you need €10k but it could be as high as €12k for some item – say so. Don't get found out when you run out of money!

See page 152.

Detailed projections

Almost an Appendix, this is where the real number-crunching is put – out-of-the-way at the back. The critical part here is your assumptions. Expect to be quizzed on these when you make a presentation of your business plan to a Local Enterprise Office or bank.

See page 154.

Almost finished

Your business plan is now almost finished – except that, just like your market research and testing of your product – you must test it in the real world.

Perform the Reality Check in the panel on the next page. Then give your plan to a few trusted friends to read through. Ask them to pick holes in it. Don't be defensive. Use their comments to improve the plan. Repeat as necessary.

A REALITY CHECK

You have finished your business plan. You are ready to submit it to your Local Enterprise Office, Enterprise Ireland or bank. Before you do, run these final checks:

Is the Executive Summary:

- Short?   ☐ YES ☐ NO
- Relevant?   ☐ YES ☐ NO
- To the point?   ☐ YES ☐ NO
- Interesting?   ☐ YES ☐ NO
- Packed with "Ooomph"?   ☐ YES ☐ NO

Check the entire business plan (get help if you need it) for:

- **Spelling mistakes:** Use a spelling checker
- **Grammatical mistakes:** Use a grammar checker (but be careful)
- **Page numbering:** Are the pages all in order, with no gaps or duplication?
- **Chapter / section numbering:** Are the chapters / sections all in order, with no gaps or duplication?
- **Cross-references between sections / pages:** Are these correct?
- **Logical structure:** Does the plan flow in a sensible order?
- **Jargon / use of language:** Do you introduce concepts, explain jargon, demystify complicated things for the reader?
- **Length:** Is it too long? Could you cut parts out, without damaging it? Could sections be moved into an Appendix?
- **Type size / style:** Is it easy to read? Are headings clearly identifiable?
- **Colour:** If you are using coloured type, does it help or does it distract? Keep it simple.

BUSINESS PLAN EXAMPLE

I EXECUTIVE SUMMARY

Use this section to write a brief summary (no more than 1 page) of the whole business plan.

II INTRODUCTION AND BACKGROUND

Explain here the purpose of the business plan. Put it in your own words.

This Business plan is written to:

- Document strategy
- Act as a management tool in monitoring performance
- Raise €___k equity funding from
- Raise €___k grant aid from
- Other (specify):

Background

Business name: Address:

Telephone / Facsimile / E-mail:

Status:

- Sole trader
- Partnership
- Limited company

Registered for:

- VAT
- PAYE / PRSI
- Corporation tax
- Income tax

Formed as:

- Purchase of existing business
- Purchase of franchise
- Start-up
- ➢ Other (specify)

Business in operation?

- Yes, started on
- No, planned to start on ___

Product / service range

Product / service	Description	Price €
A		
B		
C		
D		
E		
F		

*Copy this from **Products and Production**, page 61.*

III PROJECT OUTLINE

General description of proposed business

Trends in industry

*Copy this from **Developing a Strategy**, page 34.*

Targets
*Copy this from **Developing a Strategy**, page 34.*

IV OWNERSHIP, MANAGEMENT AND EMPLOYMENT
Founders / Management
Name: Address:
Telephone / Facsimile / E-mail: Date of birth:
Nationality: Marital status:
Percentage shareholding:
The first four sections must be completed for EACH founder or key manager. Use additional pages, if necessary.

Education

Year(s)	School / course	Degree / certificate

Work Experience

Year(s)	Organisation	Position

Other Experience
Describe other significant experience that could be useful for your business

Employer and employees
Initially, how will your staffing be organised:
- You alone, while holding another wage-earning position?
  ☐ YES ☐ NO
- You alone, full-time? ☐ YES ☐ NO
- You and your partner, full-time? ☐ YES ☐ NO
- You and your partner, part-time? ☐ YES ☐ NO
- You and your business partner(s) ? ☐ YES ☐ NO
- You and your business partner(s) with employees at a wage?
  ☐ YES ☐ NO
- How many employees full-time?
- How many employees part-time?

*Copy this from section **Staff**, page 63.*

Have you drawn up clear job descriptions for your employees?
☐ YES ☐ NO
If yes, enclose job description(s) as an Appendix.
Do you plan to expand your employee numbers quickly?
☐ YES ☐ NO
If yes, do you think you can attract enough qualified people?
☐ YES ☐ NO
Who will replace you during any required absences?

V MARKET AND MARKETING STRATEGY

Overview of the market

Describe the market in which you operate and the level of competition you face. Copy information from Marketing, page 41 onwards.

What are the leading indicators in your market sector?

- Average annual turnover per employee
- Average annual turnover per m² of selling space
- Average annual purchases per head of population
- Extent of the service area per outlet
- Other

What's your estimate of the Irish market for your product / service?

What part of this market do you intend to service?   %

Have you contacted future customers?   ☐ YES ☐ NO

What was their reaction?

Have you obtained any forward orders?   ☐ YES ☐ NO

If yes, enclose copies as an Appendix.

What comments did you receive with the forward orders?

The forward orders total approximately   €   k

Market

Who are your target groups?

What do you have to offer them?

Competitors

Competitor	Description of product / service	Turnover €	Employees
A			
B			
C			
D			
E			
F			

Competitors' strengths compared to your own.

(Use + where you think your business is better, = where they are the same, and − where you think your competitors have an advantage.)

Competitor	A	B	C	D	E	F
Broad Range						
Guarantee						
Quality						
Price						
Service						
Delivery						
Proximity						
Other						

In what ways do your products / services differ from your competitors'? (If you can, describe differences for each competitor)

A

B

C

D

E

F

Key competitive advantages

What extras do you offer compared to the competition?

A

B

C

D

E

F

Marketing strategy

How are you going to present your business?

- Layout

- Colours

- Music

- Atmosphere

- Correspondence

- Brochures

- Business cards

- Van signs

- Website

- Social media

Rate those areas your customers are most interested in, and your relative strengths in those areas.

Buying Motive	Customer Importance			Your Relative Strength		
	High	Medium	Low	Strong	OK	Weak
Broad Range						
Guarantee						
Quality						
Price						
Delivery						
Service						
Proximity						
Other						

How are you going to approach your customers and what buying motives are you going to emphasise?

What marketing and promotion resources will you emphasise?

Resource	Emphasis				Cost €
	A lot	A little	Not at all	Not yet	
Brochures					
Mailings					
Advertisements					
Sponsorship					
Word-of-mouth					
Personal selling					
Notice boards					
Public relations					
Website					
Social media					

Explain your promotion methods (how, where, frequency, why, etc.)

Distribution
How will your products / services be distributed?
Are product deliveries insured? ☐ YES ☐ NO
If yes, for how much € k
If your goods or services are supplied under standard terms of trade, summarise them here.
Enclose a copy of your full terms of trade with this plan, as an Appendix.

VI PRODUCTION
Products
Copy this from page 61.

Products / services **Description** **Price**
A
B
C

Describe your production process.
What experience do you have with this process?
Are you involved with (or will you be using) new techniques or new products in your production processes? ☐ YES ☐ NO
If yes, are you receiving assistance from experts? ☐ YES ☐ NO
If yes, who are they and how are they engaged?

New capital expenditure required?
What equipment are you using in the production process?
List the equipment you intend to lease, buy new, or buy used.

Description	New / Used?		Buy / Lease?		Cost €
	New	Used	Buy	Lease	

What guarantees do you have for this equipment in case of malfunction (re-purchase, service contract, insurance)?
Does the available production equipment provide enough capacity to achieve the revenue you have budgeted? ☐ YES ☐ NO

Quality
Will your production process be accredited to a Quality Standard?
If yes, which?
- Quality Mark
- Hygiene Mark
- ISO 9000 / 2000
- ISO 14000
- Other

Have you checked your products and production processes for environmental considerations: pollution, noise, undesirable waste products?   ☐ YES ☐ NO
If Yes, are there any environmental objections?   ☐ YES ☐ NO
If Yes, what are you planning to do about it?

Raw material sources
Have you contacted your future suppliers?   ☐ YES ☐ NO
If Yes, what are their terms of trade? (Payment conditions, delivery times, etc.)
Are there alternative suppliers?   ☐ YES ☐ NO
If Yes, list them.
What advantages do these alternative suppliers offer you?

VII FINANCIAL
Summary of projected performance
Profit and loss account
Copy this from page 122.

Revenue by product	Year 1 €	Year 2 €	Year 3 €
Cash sales			
A			
B			
C			
D			
E			
Credit sales			
A			
B			
C			
D			
E			
Total sales			
Deduct			
Opening stock			
Purchases			
Less closing stock			
Cost of Goods Sold			
Gross profit			
Gross profit %			
Overheads			
Staff			
Production			
Premises			
IT			
Transport			
Sales and promotion			
General expenses			
Finance			
Depreciation			
Total costs			
Net profit			
Less tax on profits			
Profit retained			

What effect will any shortfall in turnover have on your business and how do you plan to handle it?
What is your minimum required turnover?   €__k

Cashflow

Copy this from page 156.

	Year1 €	Year2 €	Year3 €
Opening balance			
Incoming			
Sources of finance			
Cash sales			
Debtors			
VAT refunds			
Other income			
Total income			
Outgoing			
Initial investment			
Cash purchases			
Creditors			
Overheads:			
➢ Staff			
➢ Production			
➢ Premises			
➢ IT			
➢ Transport			
➢ Selling / promo			
➢ Gen. expenses			
Finance costs			
Loan repayments			
Personal drawings			
Fixed assets			
VAT payable			
Other taxes			
Other expenses			
Total outgoings			
Net cashflow			
Closing balance			

VIII   FUNDING PROPOSAL
Funding requirements
Year 1
Copy this from page 113.

1. Fixed assets	€
Property	
Renovations	
Fixtures and fittings	
Transport	
Machines and equipment	
Goodwill, security deposits	
Other	
Total fixed assets	
2. Current assets	
Stock of raw material	
Stock of finished goods	
Work in progress	
Debtors	
Other	
Total current assets	
3. Liquid assets	
Cash	
Bank	
Other	
Total liquid assets	
Margin for unforeseen costs	
Total investment	

Proposed sources of funding
Copy this from page 114.

Personal assets available			€
Fixed assets			
Car			
Additional personal mortgage			
Savings			
Deferred loans (family)			
Other			
Total personal assets			
Introduced as:			
➢ Equity			
➢ Loans			
External equity			
➢ Source?		Agreed?	
External debt	Term (years)	Agreed?	
➢ Long / medium-term		Y / N	
➢ Mortgage			
➢ Loan			
➢ Leasing			
➢ Other			
Total			
Short-term finance			
➢ Overdraft			
➢ Suppliers' credit			
➢ Payments received in advance			
➢ Other			
Total			
Subsidies / grants			
Agency ?			
Local Enterprise Office			
Area Partnership Company			
Other			
Total subsidies / grants			
Total available finance			

Can you support the required investment in fixed assets with quotations from suppliers?   ☐ YES ☐ NO
If Yes, enclose quotations as an Appendix.
In your estimates, did you take seasonal business influences into account, and calculate based on your maximum requirements?
                                                    ☐ YES ☐ NO
How did you estimate your stock levels?
How did you estimate the value of your work-in-progress?
How did you estimate the value of your debtors?
Do you have sufficient liquid assets to cope with disappointments, delays and unexpected expenses?   ☐ YES ☐ NO

IX DETAILED PROJECTIONS
Assumptions
Copy this from page 123.

- Sales
- Purchases
- Stocks
- Staff salaries
- Production overheads
- Premises costs
- IT costs
- Transport costs
- Selling and promotion costs
- General expenses
- Finance costs

Depreciation

Analysis of Overheads
Copy this from page 120.

	Year 1 €	Year 2 €	Year 3 €
Staff costs			
Gross staff salaries			
Employer's PRSI			
Bonuses, etc.			
Staff training costs			
Other staff costs			
Total staff costs			
Production overheads			
Use of auxiliary materials			
Maintenance			
Heat, light & power			
Rent / lease equipment			
Insurance equipment			
Other costs			
Total production costs			
Premises costs			
Rent			
Heat, light & power			
Insurance			
Cleaning			
Maintenance			
Other costs			
Deduct:			
Rent received			
Total premises costs			
IT costs			
Broadband			
Website			

Consumables			
Other costs			
Total IT costs			
Transport costs			
Maintenance and repairs			
Lease costs			
Fuel			
Insurance			
Road Tax			
Public transport			
Air fares			
Deduct:			
Private use			
Total transport costs			
Selling and promotion costs			
Advertising			
Packaging			
Promotion			
Trade fairs			
Commissions			
Other costs			
Total sales and promotion costs			
General expenses			
Telephone			
Postage			
Subscriptions			
Insurance			
Stationery			
Office expenses			
Accountancy fees			
Legal & other fees			
Other costs			
Total general expenses			
Finance costs			
Interest on loans / / overdraft			
Mortgage interest			
Charges / fees			
Other			
Total finance costs			
Depreciation			
Property			
Fixtures & fittings			
Total depreciation costs			
Total costs			

Cashflow

Bring forward from pages 157-159.

	Year1 €	Year2 €	Year3 €
Opening balance			
Incoming			
Sources of finance			
Cash sales			
Debtors			
VAT refunds			
Other income			
Total income			
Outgoing			
Initial investment			
Cash purchases			
Creditors			
Overheads:			
➢ Staff			
➢ Production			
➢ Premises			
➢ IT			
➢ Transport			
➢ Selling / promo			
➢ Gen. expenses			
Finance costs			
Loan repayments			
Personal drawings			
Fixed assets			
VAT payable			
Other taxes			
Other expenses			
Total outgoings			
Net cashflow			
Closing balance			

	M1 €	M2 €	M3 €	M4 €	M5 €	M6 €	M7 €	M8 €	M9 €	M10 €	M11 €	M12 €	Year 1 Total €
Opening balance													
Incoming													
Sources of finance													
Cash sales													
Debtors													
VAT refunds													
Other income													
Total income													
Outgoing													
Initial investment													
Cash purchases													
Creditors													
Overheads:													
➤ Staff													
➤ Production													
➤ Premises													
➤ IT													
➤ Transport													
➤ Selling / promo													
➤ Gen. expenses													
Finance costs													
Loan repayments													
Personal drawings													
Fixed assets													
VAT payable													
Other taxes													
Other expenses													
Total outgoings													
Net cashflow													
Closing balance													

	M1 €	M2 €	M3 €	M4 €	M5 €	M6 €	M7 €	M8 €	M9 €	M10 €	M11 €	M12 €	Year 2 Total €
Opening balance													
Incoming													
Sources of finance													
Cash sales													
Debtors													
VAT refunds													
Other income													
Total income													
Outgoing													
Initial investment													
Cash purchases													
Creditors													
Overheads:													
➢ Staff													
➢ Production													
➢ Premises													
➢ IT													
➢ Transport													
➢ Selling / promo													
➢ Gen. expenses													
Finance costs													
Loan repayments													
Personal drawings													
Fixed assets													
VAT payable													
Other taxes													
Other expenses													
Total outgoings													
Net cashflow													
Closing balance													

	M1 €	M2 €	M3 €	M4 €	M5 €	M6 €	M7 €	M8 €	M9 €	M10 €	M11 €	M12 €	Year 3 Total €
Opening balance													
Incoming													
Sources of finance													
Cash sales													
Debtors													
VAT refunds													
Other income													
Total income													
Outgoing													
Initial investment													
Cash purchases													
Creditors													
Overheads:													
➢ Staff													
➢ Production													
➢ Premises													
➢ IT													
➢ Transport													
➢ Selling / promo													
➢ Gen. expenses													
Finance costs													
Loan repayments													
Personal drawings													
Fixed assets													
VAT payable													
Other taxes													
Other expenses													
Total outgoings													
Net cashflow													
Closing balance													

PITCHING YOUR PLAN

OBJECTIVES

o Understand the importance of presentation

o Prepare to present your business plan

Pitching to investors should now be part of the skillset of every ambitious entrepreneur, since it has almost superseded the business plan as a tool used to communicate the business proposition. Pitching to investors is about understanding what investors need to know about you and your venture and shaping that into a compelling story.

Guy Kawasaki recommends the 10 / 20 / 30 rule for presentations (see **https://guykawasaki.com/the-only-10-slides-you-need-in-your-pitch/**). That means:

- 10 slides
- 20 minutes
- 30-point font.

The 10 slides should cover:

- Title
- Problem / opportunity
- Value proposition
- Underlying magic
- Business model
- Go-to-market plan
- Competitive analysis
- Management team
- Financial projections and key metrics
- Current status, accomplishments to date, timeline and use of funds.

Some other guidelines for pitching:

- Wrap up, recap and go for the close. Tell them again in summary what your pitch story was and deliver your prepared, thought-out, aggressive-enough 'ask'
- Anticipate questions that you might be asked. Try and build the answers into your presentation, so that you have answered them before they can be asked.
- Always show progress as a team, product and with customers.
- Understand the management, market, financial, technological and operational risks to your venture and the industry it will compete in – investors will ask.
- Know the 10 companies across the different verticals who will want to acquire your venture and why – investors will ask.
- Keep the business model specific, simple and non-aggressive. It shouldn't be a total innovation.
- Understand that the deal must make lots of money for the

The minute you start talking about what you're going to do if you lose, you have lost.
GEORGE SCHULTZ

160

investor – multiples of 5 to 10 times initial capital to be earned in an exit 5 to 8 years down the line.

Finally, relax! It's your business! You know more about it than any investor, Local Enterprise Office officer or banker will ever learn. You are a self-confident, capable, well-organised entrepreneur with a good business plan. Go for it!

SMELL THE FLOWERS

- o Appreciate balance in life

Don't hurry, don't worry. You're only here for a short visit. So be sure to stop and smell the flowers.
WALTER HAGEN

TWELVE THINGS TO REMEMBER:
The value of time.
The success of perseverance.
The pleasure of working.
The dignity of simplicity.
The worth of character.
The power of kindness.
The influence of example.
The obligation of duty.
The wisdom of economy.
The virtue of patience.
The improvement of talent.
The joy of origination.
MARSHALL FIELD

Starting and running your own business is all-consuming. Everything falls back on you. And you are doing it for yourself – so there is a temptation to do too much. Certainly, it is hard (and may even be damaging to your business) to turn down work but, at some point, you need to take time out to decide what is really important to you, what you are achieving at present and what you need to do about it. This is where time management comes in.

Time management

An average working week for an entrepreneur is between 70 and 80 hours. As well as handling all aspects of the business – book-keeping, selling, clients, networking, etc. – you also must know how to handle your time and how to maintain your entrepreneurial drive.

You, the entrepreneur, are the most important success factor in the business. It is vital that this success factor is maintained. An entrepreneur needs to know when to peak and when to rest and take it easy. It is impossible to go full throttle all the time.

Go back to the first chapter, **READY**, and ask yourself how much time you are willing to spend on the business. Discuss it with your partner / spouse.

Go back to your assessment of your strong and weak points. Then go back to your market research and your identification of the critical success factors for your business.

Next, decide whether you are a morning person or an evening person. When do you function best? Whenever it is, aim to do your best work then. Start late and keep your heavy thinking till late at night if that suits – or start at six in the morning and knock off at four in the afternoon.

As an entrepreneur, you can choose your hours. Choose them to make the most of yourself.

Now some tips for managing your time:
- Make a daily "To Do list"
- Learn to say "NO"
- Protect yourself, take time off regularly
- A healthy mind in a healthy body
- Never handle documents more than once (no paper shuffling, deal with it and get it off your desk permanently)
- Keep things simple
- Do the things you hate first
- Manage your stress levels (meditate, exercise)
- Delegate

- To handle paperwork – TRAF: Toss, Refer, Act or File – only do one, and only once!

Make time for yourself

However pressured your business, you need to take some time out to unwind – to "smell the flowers". Without it, you will burn out. Add time to your diary – every day, every week, every month – for your-self. Cut yourself free from the business and the other demands on your life. Allow your batteries to recharge – and you will come back to the business better able to make it succeed.

GO!

INTRODUCTION

o Assist in establishing a business by providing sample documents

o Understand core topics relevant to the continued success and development of a business

In the earlier chapters in this guide, you:

- Assessed your own suitability (and that of your business partners) for business and decided to proceed to the next stage
- Considered all the many factors that impact on the success of a start-up – from a mission statement and strategy, through marketing, finance and budgeting – and took these into account in developing your business plan.

This chapter of the workbook takes you onwards from the business plan, into the detail of starting and running your new business.

It starts with sample documents, designed to save you time and difficulty, including:

- **Sample accounts pages**
- **Sample Job Application:** Adapt this as necessary
- **Sample Job Description:** Adapt this as necessary
- **Sample Employment Contract:** Where necessary, take professional HR or legal advice on any changes needed to this sample contract to adapt it to the circumstances of your business
- **Sample Safety Statement:** Again, where necessary, take professional advice on adapting this sample statement to the circumstances of your own business

You can download copies of these documents at **www.startingabusinessinireland.com**.

The chapter then covers topics whose importance only becomes apparent once a business is up and running. They have been touched upon in the **STEADY** chapter, but here they are considered in a little more detail. They are:

- Quality
- Environmental concerns
- Health and safety
- Intellectual property
- Cyber-security
- Monitoring performance.

However, most could fill a book on their own and so further research and reading is recommended, depending on your own specific circumstances.

Unlike the other chapters, there are no Key Questions here – just a genuine wish to see you succeed. Keep going!

COMPLETING THE ACCOUNTS PAGES

The accounts pages shown here are based on the discussion in *Accounting* in the previous chapter, **STEADY**. This section explains how to use them.

Purchases on credit

This page records all the goods and services that you buy on credit and will have to pay for later.

The core information you are recording is:

- The date – in the first column
- The type of transaction – on the top of the page (Purchases on credit)
- The other person involved – the supplier, in the second column
- The amount involved – in the third column, headed up "Total".

Next, if your business is registered for VAT, you need to analyse the Total amount for VAT purposes – between the VAT itself and the "net" amount. (If your business is not registered for VAT, ignore the fourth and fifth – VAT and Net – columns).

Last, you need to analyse your purchases across the overhead categories defined earlier. This analysis will help you manage your business better by showing how your money is being spent. Write the net amount of the transaction in one of the remaining columns – Staff, Production, Premises, Transport, Selling, General, Finance or Other – according to where it belongs.

At the end of each week, or month, depending on the number of transactions, total the page and start a new one.

Sales on credit

Sales on credit accounts for all sales that you invoice and have to wait to get paid for. You complete the page in much the same way as the Purchases on credit page.

Write the date in the first column, and the customer in the second. The total amount of the trans- action goes in the third, with a breakdown between VAT and "net" in the next two columns.

Then analyse your sales on credit across product categories to suit your information needs. Any unusual sales can go in the "Other" column.

Total the page at the end of the month and start a new one.

Receipts

It is critically important that you account for all cash coming into the business. You do this by writing all incoming cash transactions in a Receipts page. For one, the taxman will want this information and you need it anyway to protect yourself from loss.

Again, similar information is required. The date and name of the other party involved, the total amount, split between VAT and "net" where it is a new transaction (not if it has been accounted for earlier, as happens when you receive payment for sales on credit).

It is useful to know the breakdown of where cash comes from:
- Are your debtors building up or paying on time?
- How much of your business is from cash sales?
- What other sources of cash have you?

Record these in the appropriate columns.

Total the page at the end of the week or month and start a new one.

Payments

Just as it is important to record cash coming in, it's also important to record cash paid out. The Payments page helps here.

Again, date and the other party to the transaction, as well as the amount, are essential information. Again, also only account for VAT on new transactions. In some cases here, you will be paying for purchases made earlier on credit – record these in the "Suppliers" column. Other purchases made for cash should be analysed into the appropriate category.

Petty Cash

This is like the Payments page but on a smaller scale of spending. It should be totalled and checked every week, so that money does not go astray. You also should have receipts for all petty cash expenditure – set this as a habit from the very start.
Bank balance book

The operation of this page is explained in the previous chapter, in *Accounting*.

Summary

These are very simple paper-based "books", which give you the absolute basics of information that you need to control your business.

Talk to your own accountant about the specific needs of your business but always keep in mind that book-keeping is a means (to information for management purposes) not an end in itself.

Accounts pages: Purchases on Credit

Date	Supplier	Total	VAT	Net	Staff	Production	Premises	Transport	Selling	General	Financial	Other
TOTAL												

Accounts pages: Sales on Credit

Date	Customer	Total	VAT	Net	Staff	Product A	Product B	Product C	...	Service Y	Service Z	Other
TOTAL												

Accounts pages: Receipts

Date	Received from	Total	VAT	Net	Staff	Debtors	Cash Sales	Loans	Other
TOTAL									

Accounts pages: Payments

Date	Paid to	Total	VAT	Net	Suppliers	Staff	Production	Premises	Transport	Selling	General	Other
TOTAL												

Accounts pages: Petty Cash

Date	Paid to	Total	VAT	Net	Postage	Stationery	Office Expenses	Transport	Other
TOTAL									

Accounts pages: Bank Balance Book

Date	Transaction	IN	OUT	Balance
TOTAL				

JOB APPLICATION FORM

POSITION

NAME (Mr / Mrs / Miss / Ms)
ADDRESS
TELEPHONE
EMAIL
DATE OF BIRTH
STATUS   [] Single   [] Married [] Divorced   [] Separated   []
Widowed
CHILDREN (Number / Ages)
HEALTH (Illnesses / Disabilities)

EDUCATION

Years		School / course	Degree / certificate
From	To		

WORK EXPERIENCE

Years		Organisation	Position
From	To		

OTHER EXPERIENCE
Describe other significant experience that could be useful in this
position

HOBBIES / INTERESTS

OTHER INFORMATION

I wish to apply for the position of
I declare the information above to be correct to the best of my
knowledge and belief.

Signed   **Date**

JOB DESCRIPTION

POSITION

NAME
DATE APPOINTED
REPORTING TO

SUBORDINATES

CORE RESPONSIBILITY

KEY TASKS
Daily
Weekly
Monthly
Yearly

TARGETS

EMPLOYMENT CONTRACT

On company letterhead
(Name)
(Address)
(Date)

Dear

The following are the terms and conditions of your employment, which I am required to give you. Should you require clarification on any point, please feel free to ask me.

Position
You will be employed primarily as (POSITION), commencing on (DATE). A job specification for the position is attached. You will be required to be flexible in this position and to undertake such other work as may be assigned to you by the company from time to time, outside the area of your normal duties. This work may be for such subsidiary or associate companies of the company as the company may require.

Hours of work
Your normal working week will be 5 days, Monday to Friday. Your normal working hours will be XXam to XXpm on those days, with one hour for lunch. Your position may require you to work in excess of these hours from time to time, especially when deadlines have to be met.

Remuneration
You will be paid monthly in arrears by credit transfer. Your salary at commencement will be €___ pa and will be reviewed on (DATE). There is no payment for overtime. If additional responsibilities or working hours in excess of normal working hours become part of your regular work, your salary may be reviewed before the review date above.

Annual leave
The company's holiday year runs from 1 January to 31 December. Your annual holiday entitlement will be 20 working days and shall be given in accordance with the *Organisation of Working Time Act, 1997*. Your entitlement in 20XX will be XXdays. Holiday dates must be agreed in advance with the Managing Director and are subject to management discretion. Public holidays shall also be given in accordance with the *Organisation of Working Time Act, 1997*.

Maternity Leave (female staff only)
You have a statutory entitlement to Maternity Leave and Maternity Benefit as provided for under the Maternity Protection Acts and the Social Welfare Acts. You are also entitled to have your existing job, or a suitable alternative, held open for you pending your return to work following maternity leave, which is calculated as four weeks before the expected date of the birth of

your child and 22 weeks following that date. To ensure your entitlement, you must:

- Provide a letter from your doctor, certifying that you are pregnant and the expected date of birth of your child

- Write a letter to the Managing Director, stating that you are pregnant, advising the dates you intend to be absent on maternity leave and stating whether you intend to return to work following your maternity leave.

Maternity Benefit is paid by the Department of Social Protection on a weekly basis throughout your maternity leave. The amount paid is not taxable, and is based on your earnings in the previous tax year. The maximum benefit payable is currently €XX per week. In addition, you have a statutory entitlement to an additional 16 weeks' unpaid leave immediately following the end of your statutory maternity leave. No benefit is payable by the Department of Social Protection during these weeks which must be taken entirely at your own expense. You must advise the Managing Director of your intention to take this unpaid leave at least four weeks before the end of your statutory maternity leave.

Sick Pay
If you are sick and unable to attend at work, you must notify the Managing Director or another senior member of staff before 10 am on the first day of non-attendance, to advise of your absence and to state how long you expect to be absent. Medical certificates must be provided to the Managing Director for absences of more than two days.
The company will pay you your normal salary, less PAYE, PRSI and USC, for up to XX weeks' sick leave in any calendar year. You must claim Social Welfare benefits, where applicable, during such sick leave and must pay any such benefits received to the company immediately on receipt. The company reserves the right to reduce the period of paid sick leave or withdraw the scheme at any time.

Retirement
Normal retirement age is XX. A pension / No pension is payable at retirement.

Grievances
If you have a grievance in relation to any aspect of your employment, you have a right to a hearing by your immediate superior. If you are unhappy with the outcome of that hearing, you may appeal to the Managing Director. You may be accompanied by a fellow employee at this appeal meeting. Where the circumstances warrant it, you may refer your grievance directly to the Managing Director. If the matter can- not be resolved within the company, it shall be referred through procedures, which shall include, as appropriate, reference to a Rights Commissioner, the Labour Relations Commission, the Labour Court, the Employment Appeals Tribunal or the Equality Officer.

Notice of Termination
Except in circumstances justifying immediate termination of your employment by the company, you are entitled to receive XX months' notice of termination of your employment. The company

reserves the right to pay you XX months' salary in lieu of notice. Your employment may be terminated without notice for serious misconduct or unreasonable failure to carry out such duties as may be assigned to you from time to time.

You must give the company XX months' notice of your intention to terminate your employment. The company reserves the right to pay you month's salary in lieu of this period of notice.

Dismissal

The company hopes that it will not be necessary to dismiss you. However, you may be dismissed for: Incompetence or poor work performance, serious or persistent misconduct, incapacity, failure to carry out reasonable instructions, redundancy, or some other substantial reason. The following procedures will be carried out before a decision to dismiss you from the company's employment is taken:

- A full investigation will be carried out by the company. You may be suspended, with or without pay at the company's discretion, during this investigation

- You will be informed of the reasons for the proposed dismissal

- You will have a right to state your case and may be accompanied by a fellow employee at any meeting that you are asked to attend concerning your proposed dismissal.

If you wish to challenge your dismissal, it shall be referred in accordance with normal procedures to a Rights Commissioner, the Labour Court, the Labour Relations Commission or the Employment Appeals Tribunal, as appropriate.

Health and safety

The company is committed to fulfilling its obligations under applicable health and safety legislation and has prepared a Safety Statement. It is a condition of your employment that you sign the Health and Safety Statement and abide by its requirements.

On behalf of (BUSINESS NAME), I wish you well in your employment. Please sign one copy of this letter to indicate your acceptance of the terms and conditions of your employment and return it to me as soon as possible.

Signed Managing Director

I accept and agree to be bound by the above terms and conditions of employment.

Signed (EMPLOYEE)

SAFETY STATEMENT

BUSINESS NAME:
ADDRESS:
BUSINESS ACTIVITY:

NAME / TEL NO of:

Doctor:	Ambulance:
Hospital:	Fire:
Gardai:	First Aider:
Safety Rep:	HSA:

This Safety Statement is aimed at protecting our employees from workplace accidents and ill-health at work. It is our programme in writing to manage health and safety. We provide protective equipment, guards, etc., as well as information, training and supervision necessary to protect our employees. The Safety Statement is available to our employees, outside contractors and inspectors of the Health and Safety Authority. We will update it as necessary and it will be reviewed at least once a year.

Signed: (Proprietor / Manager)   **Date:**

CHECKLIST OF HAZARDS AND RELATED ISSUES
Is your workplace safe, clean and tidy?
Are your work systems safe?
Is your equipment and machinery safe (guarded if necessary and maintained regularly)?
Are machinery and equipment suppliers' instructions followed?
Is portable equipment (such as ladders, welders, electrical tools, etc.) properly maintained?
Are boilers, air receivers, lifts and cranes examined and maintained?
Can manual lifting, pushing, pulling or dragging of heavy weights be avoided?
Is care taken with chemicals? Remember to read the labels and chemical safety sheets.
Are there health hazards – processes giving rise to dust or fumes?
Have you made arrangements for emergencies and fire-fighting?
Are escape routes clear?
Is there safe means of access to heights?
Are goods safely stacked?
Is there training, consultation, information and supervision of employees in health and safety?
Are records kept of safety training?
Is ventilation adequate?
Is personal protective equipment provided and used?
Do your VDUs comply with safety standards?
Are First Aid provisions adequate?
Is there any history of accidents / ill-health in the business?
Are accidents reported to the Health and Safety Authority?
Are there any other hazards in the workplace?
Are employees adhering to all remedial steps to avoid injury?
Are the welfare facilities (toilets / washing / eating / drink) adequate?
Are employees and outside contractors aware of this Safety Statement?
Have you displayed your Health and Safety poster?
Reproduced by permission of the Health and Safety Authority

QUALITY

o Understand the importance of quality

o Be aware of quality standards

Quality is in – big time! Quality has always been important as a means of differentiating products and delivering higher value-added but there is no escaping the current management focus on quality as a means of achieving higher profits through customer satisfaction.

What is quality?

Quality is an attitude of mind that results in everyone in a business working together towards:

- Eliminating (or minimising) errors and faults
- Meeting deadlines
- Mapping out clear lines of responsibility
- Continuous improvement.

Think about what quality means to you. What does it mean for your customer? What does it mean for your product / service? Write down your answers.

Quality systems

Quality systems help ensure that quality is delivered every time.

Quality certification provides independent assurance that the quality systems meet approved standards. Surveys show that quality assurance marks / logos give customers valued guidance when buying products and services and influence their decision to buy at point of sale. However, too few companies trading in Ireland have either the Q-Mark or ISO 9000 certification.

Quality standards

The key quality standards in Ireland are:

- **The Q-Mark:** Excellence Ireland Quality Association's most successful programme to date and one of the most coveted brands on the Irish market. The Q-Mark is regarded as the national symbol of quality and is essentially a framework through which a business can continually improve
- **Hygiene Mark Certification**
- **The Triple Hygiene Mark**
- **ISO 9000:** The Quality Standard, the most successful international standard ever produced and currently in use in over 70 countries world-wide
- **ISO 14000:** The Environmental Standard.

It goes without saying that your product is top quality.
HARRY CROSBIE, on developing a brand

Quality is no longer a competitive advantage. It is a minimum entry requirement in any market.
BRIAN TRACY

The Q-Mark

The Quality Systems Q-Mark is a systems and processes framework used to help continuously improve the practices that underpin the way an organisation operates. As well as giving internal confidence to organisations, enabling them to consistently deliver good product / s and / or services, the Q-Mark also enhances the organisation and its products as a brand, thus sustaining customer confidence.

The granting of the Q-Mark is based on a two-fold assessment of an organisation's quality system. First, the business completes a questionnaire from Excellence Ireland Quality Association (EIQA), which evaluates the quality system. This is followed by an in-depth, interactive, on-site audit of the system. The business is audited annually to ensure that its operations and systems are being improved upon.

The Q-Mark is only given to organisations that demonstrate to EIQA's independent auditors that their standards of quality management are rigorous and consistent. Benefits include:

- Increased management control through service delivery system
- A constructive audit
- Public recognition through display of the Q-Mark logo
- Motivational impact on employees
- Deepened understanding of customer needs and requirements
- Independent feedback to assist the organisation's development.

The Hygiene Mark

The Hygiene Mark is awarded to those organisations that have successfully completed an audit against the requirements of the EIQA Hygiene and Food Safety Programme Technical Standard.

The EIQA Hygiene and Food Safety Programme provides a framework for ensuring that organisations are meeting and exceeding legal requirements for food safety management whilst also providing guidance on continuous improvement and best practice. The Hygiene and Food Safety Programme encompasses emerging standards, codes and legal requirements in hygiene and food safety, both in Ireland and internationally.

ISO 9000

ISO 9001: 2008 is a strategic management tool, facilitating effective control over design, manufacturing and service delivery processes. Applying an ISO 9001 system for Quality Management within an organisation can result in significant benefits, including:

- **Management effectiveness:** Through structured, organised and defined authorities, responsibilities and reporting structures

- **Operating efficiency:** Through clearly documented practices and procedures
- **Cost reduction:** Through the identification and elimination of potential system deficiencies and product failures
- **Increased marketability:** Through the identification of a registered company with a quality philosophy and international standard
- **Customer satisfaction:** Through the receipt of enhanced service or product quality levels.

As ISO 9001 is a harmonised European and international standard, certification to the standard opens up international markets to companies where previously technical trade barriers may have been a major impediment.

ISO 9001 requires an organisation to implement a documented quality management system addressing all organisational activities from the definition of its quality policy and objectives to the detailing of various methodologies and controls applicable to its service delivery or product manufacturing processes. This takes the form of a Quality Manual, supported by procedures manuals, work instructions, etc. defining:

- The processes in the organisation
- The inter-relationship between the process and the customer / stakeholder
- The criteria by which the effectiveness of each process can be judged
- The activities within each process (What, Who, When and How)
- The methodologies for process improvement processes and corrective action

The business' Quality Manual is assessed to ensure that it adequately and completely conforms to the requirements of the relevant standard. The assessment is conducted on the applicant's premises by an experienced team of assessors. On approval, the business is awarded 'Registered Firm' status and can use the mark on advertising material, letterheads and for other promotional purposes. Once registered, on-going inspections ensure that quality standards are maintained.

ISO 14000

ISO 14001:2004 is a standard for the management of the environment and a business' relationship with it. It is applicable to processes of any size and is ideal for managing more complex activities within a regulatory framework (such as IPPC licensing).

ENVIRONMENTAL CONCERNS

As explained in *Developing a Strategy* in the **STEADY** chapter, customers increasingly expect companies to be concerned about their impact on the environment, both socially and physically. At the same time, EU regulations on environmental issues are becoming stricter.

Businesses tend to react in three ways:

- **Do nothing:** Wait to be pushed into complying with emerging regulations

- **Act now:** Identify potential environmental hazards and take steps to eliminate them. Use this as a "competitive edge"

- **Act for the future:** Identify new businesses that will be created by these trends and get in first.

Areas to consider include:

- Materials used, both in manufacture and packaging (toxic, recyclable, replaceable)

- Machines used

- Odour

- Noise

- Risks (health, fire, etc.)

- Waste.

In the meantime, control over the impact of your activities on the environment is an important part of the management of your business. There are, of course, legal requirements in this area, but more than that, good environmental management can lead to cost savings, enhanced customer relations and a positive product image. If you are interested in exporting your product, you will find that compliance with an environmental management standard is invaluable, especially when dealing with other European businesses.

And, more generally, businesses should be looking at their carbon footprint - customers increasingly are doing so when selecting suppliers.

Environmental Protection Agency

The Environmental Protection Agency was established under the Environmental Protection Agency Act, 1992. The Agency has a wide range of statutory duties and powers. Its main responsibilities include:

- The licensing and regulation of large / complex industrial and other processes with significant polluting potential, on the basis of integrated pollution control (IPC) and the application of best available technologies for this purpose

- The monitoring of environmental quality, including the establishment of databases to which the public will have access, and the publication of periodic reports on the state of the environment

- Advising public authorities in respect of environmental functions and assisting local authorities in the performance of their environmental protection functions

- The promotion of environmentally sound practices through, for example, the encouragement of the use of environmental audits, the setting of environmental quality objectives and the issuing of codes of practice on matters affecting the environment

- The promotion and co-ordination of environmental research

- The licensing and regulation of all significant waste recovery activities, including landfills and the preparation and updating periodically of a national hazardous waste plan for implementation by other bodies

- Generally overseeing the performance by local authorities of their statutory environmental protection functions.

Environmental management systems

An environmental management system can take many forms – for example:

- **IS EN ISO 14001:** Published by the NSAI

- **ISO 14000:** See *Quality Certification*

- **Self-audited systems:** Such as that outlined in *A guide to environmental self-auditing* published by the Chambers of Commerce in Ireland

- **EU Eco-Management & Audit Scheme.**

HEALTH AND SAFETY

Health and safety in the workplace has become a major issue in industry in recent years, driven largely by EU regulations and by an increasing awareness of employers' social responsibilities. Put simply, an employer is responsible in so far as is reasonably practicable for the safety, health and welfare of his / her employees. Employees also have a duty to ensure their own health and safety as well as that of other staff and others in the workplace.

o Understand the law relating to health and safety

o Understand the application of health and safety in your workplace

Safety, Health & Welfare at Work Act, 2005

This updated Act applies to all places of work, regardless of size or activity, all employers and self-employed persons, manufacturers, suppliers and importers.

Under the Act, an employer must:

- Consult with employees on health and safety issues and allow employees to select a Safety Representative to represent them in these discussions

- Prepare a Safety Statement, which outlines the hazards identified in the place of work and details how they are controlled in order to safeguard the health and safety of employees

- Ensure that working practices and procedures, means of access and exit, and articles or substances used at the workplace or provided for use at work are safe and not dangerous to employees' health. This duty extends beyond the company's own employees to include employees of other businesses who happen to be in the workplace

- Test plant, equipment or materials he / she manufactures, designs, imports or supplies and give adequate information on associated hazards.

Other legislation

Where the 2005 Act forms the skeleton, the detail is provided by the Safety, Health and Welfare at Work (General Application) Regulations, 2006 and other industry-specific legislation.

Areas covered include:

- Risk assessment
- Design of the workplace
- Use of work equipment
- Manual handling methods
- Use of visual display units
- Electricity

- Protective equipment
- The availability of first aid
- Notification of accidents and dangerous occurrences.

Specific legislation covers hazards such as noise, chemicals and certain named substances, asbestos, lead, infection, and biological risks, safety signs and conditions for pregnant employees, etc.

The Health & Safety Authority has a range of publications that provide guidance on the Act and subsequent regulations, though industry-specific legislation is outside its remit.

The Health & Safety Authority

The Health and Safety Authority (HSA) is the national body in Ireland with responsibility for securing health and safety at work, in every type of workplace and every kind of work in the public and private sectors.

Its functions include:

- Providing advice and information
- Promoting safety
- Undertaking research
- Enforcing health and safety laws generally.

HSA inspectors may visit any workplace at any time to inspect documents, books, registers, and the physical environment.

A range of enforcement mechanisms may be used, such as improvement directions, plans and notices and prohibition notices.

INTELLECTUAL PROPERTY

Patents

A patent is an exclusive right given by the State and enforceable in the Courts. It gives the "patentee" a monopoly to make, use and sell the invention for a fixed period of time and the right to stop others manufacturing, using or selling the patented invention during that period unless they have obtained the patent owner's authorisation to do so. In return for this monopoly, the patentee pays fees to cover the costs of processing the patent application and granting the patent. Annual renewal fees are also paid in order to keep the patent in force. A patent can last for 10 years (short term) or 20 years. A patent granted in Ireland gives no rights in other countries.

To be eligible for the grant of a valid patent, an invention must be new, involve an inventive step and be capable of industrial application.

Not all inventions qualify for the grant of a patent. The *Patents Act, 1992* specifically excludes:

- A discovery, scientific theory or a mathematical method
- An aesthetic creation
- A scheme rule or method for performing a mental act, playing a game or doing business or a programme for a computer
- The presentation of information
- Methods of treatment of the human or animal body by surgery or therapy
- Plant and animal varieties or essentially biological processes for their production
- Inventions that are contrary to public order or morality.

European Patents

The European Convention (EPC) came into force in 1977 and established the European Patent Office (EPO). A European patent application can be filed either with the Irish Patents Office or directly with The Hague Branch of the EPO and the applicant can choose to designate any of the 18 contracting states including Ireland. When granted, a European patent has the effect of a national patent in each of the countries designated. Therefore, an applicant may find it considerably cheaper to lodge a single patent application to the EPO, designating a number of contracting states, as opposed to lodging individual patent applications with each of the countries.

Inventors are warned that it is unwise to make any public disclosure of an invention or to put it into use publicly before an application for a patent has been made, as such action may prejudice the obtaining of a valid patent.
THE PATENTS OFFICE

Patent Co-operation Treaty (PCT)

The Patent Co-operation Treaty (PCT) came into effect in 1978. Its main aim is to streamline patent application filing and novelty search procedures for applicants wishing to obtain patent protection in a wide number of countries around the world. The PCT provides a system whereby a single international application in one of the contracting states allows for the designation of up to 80 other countries in which one wishes to have patent protection. The applicant designates those in which a patent is desired and eventually the relevant national authority may grant a patent. The Patents Office acts as a receiving office for PCT applications.

Trade Marks

Once a business has a product to sell, it needs something which distinguishes its goods and services from those of competitors. A trade mark is a sign which is capable of being represented graphically (in words or pictures written down) and which is capable of distinguishing the goods or services of one business from those of other businesses. It may consist of words (including personal names), designs, letters, numerals, or the shape of the goods or of their packaging. An applicant is required to pay fees to register a trade mark and renewal fees to keep it in force.

The *Trade Marks Act, 1996* allows the registration of a trade mark for a service.

A trade mark should be distinctive, not deceptive, not descriptive and not among certain excluded items listed in the Act (such as national emblems, immoral or offensive language).

When registered, a trade mark is valid for 10 years from the application date and may be renewed every 10 years.

You apply for trademark registration to:
- (For Ireland) Patents Office, Government Buildings, Hebron Road, Kilkenny
- (For EU) Office for Harmonisation in the Internal Market, Avenida de Europa 4, Apartado de Correos 77, E-03080, Alicante, Spain.

Industrial Designs

A design is a new idea or a conception of the external "shape, configuration, pattern or ornament" intended to be assumed by any article. Designs may be registered in respect of such diverse items as toys, lamps, articles of furniture, containers, clothes, fabrics and wallpaper.

A design applied to an article should not be confused with what may be a patentable invention, or a "device" trademark (a trademark containing or consisting of a picture or drawing). A trade mark is only used for the purpose of indicating the origin of the goods / service on which it is used.

To be eligible for registration, a design must be new or original and must not have been published previous to the application. A design may be registered initially for five years and may be renewed for further periods of five years, subject to a maximum of 15 years.

The *Industrial Designs Act, 2001* updated and enhanced Irish industrial design law, broadening the civil and criminal remedies available in respect of infringements of design rights, implementing the EU Directive on the legal protection of designs and enabling future access for Irish designs to an international system of design protection under the Geneva Act of The Hague Agreement.

Copyright Protection

Copyright is the creator's (or legal owner's) rights in creative works like paintings, writings, computer software, photographs, drawings, sound recordings, films and television broadcasts. No formality such as registration or deposit of the work or payment of fees is required in order that copyright may subsist in a work.

The author of a work is the first owner of copyright in the work, except in the case of a work made under a contract of service in the course of employment. Subject to any agreement with the author, copyright in Government publications belongs to the Government. To avoid others copying your work, it is essential to be able to show proof of ownership. It is advisable for an author to sign, date and witness his / her work as proof of ownership and to display the international copyright symbol © prominently on his / her work.

The law relating to copyright was updated by the *Copyright and Related Rights Act, 2000*. This is a complex area, and it is advisable to seek legal advice on any matter of doubt or dispute.

Information and Advice

The Patent Office has a library at its Kilkenny offices, containing various legal and technical reference works which may be of interest to inventors. In addition to providing access to a wide range of patent and trademark information in paper form, the Library also offers some electronic patent information services through CD-ROM computer terminals and also provides a document delivery service to the public.

The laws relating to intellectual property are complex and it is advisable for intending applicants to consult a registered patent or trade mark agent in advance. Application forms, information leaflets and lists of registered patent / trademark agents are available from the Patents Office (**www.patentsoffice.ie**).

CYBER-SECURITY

The risks to any business, however small, from cyber-attacks is growing daily – just read the business press. And the consequences can be devastating – for your business and for your customers whose security also has been compromised.

No system of cyber-security can be 100% secure but, with a little commonsense, simple, practical and inexpensive measures can be put in place to reduce the risk.

The UK Information Commissioner's Office publishes *A Practical Guide to IT Security*, which is intended for use by small businesses. Although primarily focused on protection of personal data, it suggests 10 commonsense steps to manage security in your business:

- Assess the threats and risks to your business
- Get in line with Cyber Essentials – see below
- Secure data on the move and in the office
- Secure your data in the cloud
- Back up your data
- Train staff
- Keep an eye out for problems
- Know what you should be doing
- Minimise your data
- Make sure your IT contractor is doing what they should be

The Cyber Essentials scheme recommends:
- Boundary firewalls and internet gateways
- Secure configuration
- Access control
- Malware protection
- Patch management and software updates.

Remember, it's not just the computer systems on your premises that are at risk / vulnerable. Consider also the laptops and tablets that you or your staff might use off-premises, accessing your network over insecure public networks in a coffee shop perhaps, and their own computers when they are working from home. And last, smartphones are computers too!

So anti-virus software is essential, as is password control (please don't tape your password to the bottom of your keyboard!). Encryption of data on computers – especially portable devices – is another useful step. But, most important, is a wary attitude.

MONITORING PERFORMANCE

It is important that you monitor the progress of your business against your business plan forecasts on a quarterly, monthly, even weekly basis. If you do not, there is a danger that things will go wrong without you knowing about it. In particular, if you do not watch your cash-flow carefully, you could run into difficulties very quickly.

Most lenders are keen to have regular financial information on the performance of the businesses to which they lend money. How they get it depends on the local manager and the arrangements he makes, since few small businesses have the capacity or ability to supply monthly or quarterly accounts.

The panel provides a simple system both for you to monitor the financial performance of your business and to communicate it to your bank manager.

The first column is taken from your business plan and represents your forecast performance. The second is your actual performance to date, which you will get from your accounts. Calculate the difference between budget and actual, both in money and in percentages.

OBJECTIVES

o Understand the importance of monitoring performance

o Be aware of monitoring techniques

WHAT STAGE IS YOUR BUSINESS AT?

Existence and survival
Owner is business
Problem is finding customers and cashflow
Consolidation and control
Developing systems
Problem is to generate repeat sales and financial control
Control and planning
Taking on staff
Focus on management
Problem is fighting competition, development of new markets and control of margins and costs
Expansion
Delegation and decentralisation
Market expansion (new products and / or markets)
Tight financial control

If it's working, keep doing it.
If it's not working, stop doing it.
If you don't know what to do, don't do anything.
MEDICAL SCHOOL ADVICE

MONITORING PERFORMANCE

Month / Quarter / Year ended …

Product	Revenue for Month / Quarter / Year ended …			
	Budget €	Actual €	Difference %	Comment
A				
B				
C				
D				
E				
F				
Total revenue				
Gross profit				
Gross profit % of turnover				
Staff costs				
Production costs				
Premises				
IT				
Transport costs				
Sales and promotion				
General expenses				
Finance costs				
Depreciation				
Total overheads				
Net profit				
Net cashflow				

APPENDIX 1: SOURCES OF ASSISTANCE

ACCA Europe, 9 Leeson Park, Dublin 6 E: info@accaglobal.com W: www.accaglobal.com/ie

ACT Venture Capital Ltd, 6 Richview Office Park, Clonskeagh, Dublin 14 T: (01) 260 0966 E: info@actvc.ie W: www. actventure.com

AIB Bank, Bankcentre, Ballsbridge, Dublin 4 W: aib.ie

AIB Seed Capital Fund, Dublin Business Innovation Centre, The Tower, Trinity Enterprise Centre, Pearse Street, Dublin 2 T: (01) 671 3111 E: info@dublinbic.ie W: www.dublinbic.ie

Amárach Research, 11 Kingswood Business Centre, Kingswood Road, Citywest Campus, Dublin D24 KT63 T: (01) 410 5200 E: info@amarach.com

Arts Council, 70 Merrion Square, Dublin D02 NY52 T: (01) 618 0200 E: reception@artscouncil.ie W: www.artscouncil.ie

Balbriggan Enterprise Development Group, Unit 9, The BEAT Centre, Stephenstown Industrial Estate, Balbriggan, Co Dublin T: (01) 802 0417 E: info@bedg.ie W: www.bedg.ie

Ballyfermot Chapelizod Partnership, 4 Drumfinn Park, Ballyfermot, Dublin 10 T: (01) 623 5612 E: info@ballyfermotpartnership.ie W: www.ballyfermotpartnership.ie

Ballymun Whitehall Area Partnership, North Mall, Ballymun Shopping Centre, Dublin 11 T: (01) 842 3612 E: info@ballymun.org W: www. ballymun.org

Bank of Ireland Business Banking, W: businessbanking.bankofireland.com

Bank of Ireland Kernel Capital Partners Venture Funds, Rubicon Centre, Rossa Avenue, Bishopstown, Cork T: (021) 492 8974 E: n.olden@kernelcapital.ie W: www.kernelcapital.ie

Blanchardstown Area Partnership, Dillon House, 106 Coolmine Business Park,

Dublin 15 T: (01) 820 9550 E: info@bap.ie W: www.bap.ie

Bolton Trust, 128-130 East Wall Road, Dublin 3 T: (01) 240 1377 E: info@docklandsinnovation.ie W: www.docklandsinnovation.ie

Bord Bia — The Irish Food Board, Clanwilliam Court, Lower Mount Street, Dublin D02 A344 T: (01) 668 5155 E: info@bordbia.ie W: www.bordbia.ie

Bord Iascaigh Mhara — Irish Sea Fisheries Board, PO Box 12, Crofton Road, Dun Laoire, Co Dublin A96 E5A0 T: (01) 214 4100 E: sullivan@bim.ie W: www.bim.ie

Bplans.com W: www.bplans.com

Bray Area Partnership, 4 Prince of Wales Terrace, Quinsboro Road, Bray, Co Wicklow T: (01) 286 8266 E: info@brayareapartnership.ie W:www. brayareapartnership.ie

Breffni Integrated, Unit 6A Corlurgan Business Park, Ballinagh Road, Cavan H12 DP86T: (049) 433 1029 E: info@breffniint.ie W: www.breffniint.ie

Business Information Centre, Dublin City Public Library, ILAC Centre, Henry Street, Dublin D01 DY80 T: (01) 873 4333 F: (01) 872 1451 E: businesslibrary@dublincity.ie W: http://www.dublincity.ie/main-menu-services-recreation-culture-dublin-city-public-libraries-and-archive-locations-hours-1

Canal Communities Partnership, Oblate View, 2nd Floor, Tyrconnell Road, Inchicore, Dublin 8 T: (01) 473 2196 E: info@canalpartnership.com W: www.canalpartnership.com

Central Statistics Office, Skehard Road, Mahon, Cork T12 X00E T: (021) 453 5000 E: information@ cso.ie W: www.cso.ie

Centre for Co-operative Studies, O'Rahilly Building, University College Cork, Cork T: (021) 490 2570 E:

foodbusiness@ucc.ie W: www.ucc.ie/en/ccs/

Chambers Ireland, 3rd Floor, Newmount House, Lower Mount Street, Dublin 2 T: (01) 400 4300 E: info@chambers.ie W: www.chambers.ie

Chartered Accountants Ireland, Chartered Accountants House, 47 Pearse Street, Dublin 2 T: (01) 637 7200 E: ca@charteredaccountants.ie W: www.charteredaccountants.ie

Co-operative Development Society Ltd, Dominick Court, 41 Lower Dominick Street, Dublin 1 T: (01) 873 3199 E: coopsoc@eircom.net

Companies Registration Office, Bloom House, Gloucester Place Lower, Dublin 1 T: (01) 804 5200 E: info@cro.ie W: www.cro.ie Postal address: O'Brien Road, Carlow

Cork Business Innovation Centre, NSC Campus, Mahon, Cork T: (021) 230 7005 E: info@corkbic.com W: www.corkbic.com

Cork City Local Enterprise Office, Cork City Council, City Hall, Cork T: (021) 496 1828 E: info@leo.corkcity.ie W: www.localenterprise.ie/corkcity

Cork City Partnership Ltd, Heron House, Blackpool Park, Cork T: (021) 430 2310 E: info@partnershipcork.ie W: www.corkcitypartnership.ie

Cork Institute of Technology, Rossa Avenue, Bishopstown, Cork T12 P928 T: (021) 432 6100 E: info@cit.ie W: www.cit.ie

CPLN Area Partnership, Unit D, Nangor Road Business Park, Nangor Road, Clondalkin, Dublin 22 T: (01) 450 8788 E: reception@cpln.ie W: www.clondalkinpartnership.ie

Delta Partners, Media House, South County Business Park, Leopardstown, Dublin 18 T: (01) 294 0870 E: info@deltapartners.com W: www.deltapartners.com

Department of Agriculture, Food & the Marine, Agriculture House, Kildare Street, Dublin D02 WK12 T: (01) 607 2000 E: info@agriculture.gov.ie W: www.agriculture.gov.ie

Department of Housing, Planning, Community and Local Government, Custom House, Dublin D01 W6X0 T: (01) 888 2000 W: www.housing.gov.ie

Department of Jobs, Enterprise & Innovation, Head Office, 23 Kildare Street, Dublin D02 TD30 T: (01) 631 2121 E: info@djei.ie W: www.djei.ie

Department of Social Protection, Information Services, College Road, Sligo T: (071) 919 3302 W: www.welfare.ie

Design & Crafts Council of Ireland, Castle Yard, Kilkenny T: (056) 776 1804 E: emer@dccoi.ie W: www.dccoi.ie

DIT Hothouse Technology Transfer Office, Aungier Street, Dublin D02 HW71 T: (01) 402 7179 E: hothouse@dit.ie W: www.dit.ie/hothouse

Donegal Local Development Company, 1 Millennium Court, Pearse Road, Letterkenny, Co Donegal F92 W50R T: (091) 27056 E: info@dldc.org W: www.dldc.org

Dublin Business Innovation Centre, 1st Floor, The Tower, Trinity Technology & Enterprise Centre, Grand Canal Quay, Dublin 2 T: (01) 671 3111 E: startup@dublinbic.ie W: www.dublinbic.ie

Dublin North West Area Partnership, Rosehill House, Finglas Road, Dublin 11 W: www.dnwap.ie

Enterprise Equity, The Media Cube, Kill Avenue, Dun Laoire, Co Dublin T: (01) 214 5606 E: info@enterpriseequity.ie W: www.enterpriseequity.ie

Enterprise Ireland, The Plaza, East Point Business Park, Dublin D03 E5R6 T: (01) 727 2000 E: client.service@enterprise-ireland.com W: www.enterprise-ireland.com

Environmental Protection Agency, PO Box 3000, Johnstown Castle Estate, Co Wexford Y35 W821 T: (053) 916 0600 E: info@epa.ie W: www.epa.ie

Europa, W: europa.eu

European Commission Representation in Ireland, Europe House, 12-14 Lower Mount Street, Dublin 2 T: (01) 634 1111 E: eu-ie-info-request@ec.europa.eu W: ec.europa.eu/ireland/

Excellence Ireland Quality Association, Q Mark House, 68 Pembroke Road, Ballsbridge, Dublin D04 A3T6 T: (01) 660 4100 E: info@eiqa.com W: www.eiqa.com

Fáilte Ireland, 88-95 Amiens Street, Dublin D01 WR86 T: (01) 884 7700 E: customersupport@failteireland.ie W: www.failteireland.ie

Food Product Development Centre, Dublin Institute of Technology, Cathal Brugha Street, Dublin 1 T: (01) 814 6080 E: fpdc@dit.ie W: www.fpdc.dit.ie

Food Safety Authority of Ireland, Abbey Court, Lower Abbey Street, Dublin D01 W2H4 T: (01) 817 1300 E: info@fsai.ie W: www.fsai.ie

Fountain Healthcare Partners Fund, Guild House, 4th Floor, Guild Street, IFSC, Dublin D01 K2C5 T: (01) 522 5100 E: info@fh-partners.com W: www.fh-partners.com

Galway City Partnership, 3 The Plaza, Headford Road, Galway T: (091) 773466 E: info@gcp.ie W: www.gcp.ie

Galway Rural Development Company, Mellows Campus, Athenry, Co Galway T: (091) 844335 E: grd@grd.ie W: www.grd.ie

Galway–Mayo Institute of Technology, Dublin Road, Galway H91 T8NW T: (091) 753161 E: info@gmit.ie W: www.gmit.ie

Government Publications, T: (01) 647 6834 E: publications@opw.ie W: www.opw.ie/en/governmentpublications/

Guaranteed Irish Ltd, 1 Fitzwilliam Place, Dublin 2 T: (01) 661 2607 F: (01) 661 2633 E: info@guaranteedirish.ie W: www.guaranteedirish.ie

Guinness Enterprise Centre, Taylor's Lane, Dublin 8 T: (01) 410 0600 E: startup@gec.ie W: www.gec.ie

Health & Safety Authority, The Metropolitan Building, James Joyce Street, Dublin D01 K0Y8 T: (01) 614 2000 E: wcu@hsa.ie W: www.hsa.ie

IBEC, Confederation House, 84–86 Lower Baggot Street, Dublin 2 T: (01) 605 1500 E: info@ibec.ie W: www.ibec.ie

IDA Ireland, Wilton Park House, Wilton Place, Dublin 2 T: (01) 603 4000 E: idaireland@ida.ie W: www.idaireland.com

IE Domain Registry Ltd, 2 Harbour Square, Crofton Road, Dún Laoire, Co Dublin A96 D6RO T: (01) 236 5400 E: customerrelations@iedr.ie W: www.iedr.ie

Inishowen Development Partnership, St Mary's Road, Buncrana, Co Donegal T: (074) 936 2218 E: admin@inishowen.ie W: www.inishowen.ie

Institute of Certified Public Accountants in Ireland, 17 Harcourt Street, Dublin 2 T: (01) 425 1000 E: cpa@cpaireland.ie W: www.cpaireland.ie (Business Section)

Institute of Directors in Ireland, Europa House, Harcourt Street, Dublin 2 T: (01) 411 0010 E: info@iodireland.ie W: www.iodireland.ie

Institute of Management Consultants & Advisers, 51-52 Fitzwilliam Square West, Dublin 2 T: (01) 634 9636 E: info@imca.ie W: www.imca.ie C: Tom Moriarty, Development Director

Institute of Technology Carlow, Kilkenny Road, Carlow T: (059) 917 5000 E: info@itcarlow.ie W: www.itcarlow.ie

Institute of Technology Sligo, Ash Lane, Sligo F91 YW50 T: (071) 931 8510 E: info@itsligo.ie W: www. itsligo.ie

Institute of Technology Tralee, Clash, Tralee, Co Kerry T: (066) 714 5600 E: info@ittralee.ie W: www.ittralee.ie

International Fund for Ireland, PO Box 2000, Dublin 2 T: (01) 408 2130 W: www.internationalfundforireland.com

Invent, Dublin City University, Glasnevin, Dublin 9 T: (01) 700 7777 E: info@invent.dcu.ie W: www.dcu.ie/invent/index.shtml

IRD Duhallow Ltd, James O'Keeffe Institute, Newmarket, Co Cork T: (029) 60633 E: duhallow@eircom.net W: www.irdduhallow.com

IRD Kiltimagh, Aiden Street, Kiltimagh, Co Mayo T: (094) 938 1494 E:

reception@ird-kiltimagh.ie W:
www.ird-kiltimagh.ie

Irish Co-operative Society Ltd, The
Plunkett House, 84 Merrion Square,
Dublin D02 T882 T: (01) 676 4783 E:
info@icos.ie W: www.icos.ie

Irish Exporters Association, 28 Merrion
Square North, Dublin 2 T: (01) 661
2182 E: iea@irishexporters.ie W:
www.irishexporters.ie

Irish Internet Association, The Digital
Hub, 157 Thomas Street, Dublin 8 T:
(01) 542 4154 E: members@iia.ie W:
www.iia.ie

Irish League of Credit Unions, 33-41
Lower Mount Street, Dublin 2 T: (01)
614 6700 E: info@creditunion.ie W:
www.creditunion.ie

Irish Local Development Network, Tait
Business centre, Dominic Street,
Limerick T: (061) 404923 E:
info@ildn.ie W: www.ildn.ie

Irish Small and Medium Enterprises
Association, 17 Kildare Street, Dublin 2
T: (01) 662 2755 E: info@isme.ie W:
www.isme.ie

ITT Dublin, Tallaght, Dublin 24 T: (01)
404 2000 E: info@ittdublin.ie W:
www.ittdublin.ie

Kernel Capital Partners, Rubicon Centre,
Rossa Avenue, Bishopstown, Cork T:
(021) 492 8974 W:
www.kernelcapital.ie

Law Society of Ireland, Blackhall Place,
Dublin D07 VY24 T: (01) 672 4800 E:
general@lawsociety.ie W:
www.lawsociety.ie

Leitrim Development Company, Church
Street, Drumshambo, Co Leitrim T:
(071) 964 1770 E: info@ldco.ie W:
www.ldco.ie

Local Enterprise Offices W:
www.localenterprise.ie
- Carlow T: (059) 912 9783 E:
  enterprise@carlowcoco.ie W:
  www.localenterprise.ie/carlow
- Cavan T: (049) 437 7200 E:
  localenterprise@cavancoco.ie W:
  www.localenterprise.ie/cavan
- Clare, T: (065) 682 1616 E:

localenterprise@clarecoco.ie W:
www.localenterprise.ie / clare
- Cork North & West, T: (022) 43235 E:
  northcork@leo.corkcoco.ie / T: (023)
  883 4700 E: westcork@leo.corkcoco.ie
  W:
  www.localenterprise.ie/corknorthandwe
  st
- Donegal T: (074) 916 0735 E:
  info@leo.donegalcoco.ie W:
  www.localenterprise.ie/donegal
- Dublin City, T: (01) 222 5611 E:
  info@leo.dublincoco.ie W:
  www.localenterprise.ie / dublincity
- Dublin South T: (01) 414 9000 E:
  info@leo.sdublincoco.ie W:
  www.localenterprise.ie/southdublin
- Dun Laoghaire-Rathdown, T: (01) 204
  7083 E: contact@leo.dlrcoco.ie W:
  www.localenterprise.ie/DLR
- Fingal, T: (01) 890 0800 E:
  info@leo.fingal.ie W:
  www.localenterprise.ie/fingal
- Galway T: (091) 509090 E:
  info@leo.galwaycoco.ie W:
  www.localenterprise.ie/galway
- Kerry, T: (066) 718 3522 E:
  leo@kerrycoco.ie W:
  www.localenterprise.ie/kerry
- Kildare, T: (045) 980 838 E:
  localenterprise@kildarecoco.ie W:
  www.localenterprise.ie/kildare
- Kilkenny, 42 Parliament Street,
  Kilkenny T: (056) 775 2662 E:
  info@leo.kilkennycoco.ie W:
  www.localenterprise.ie/kilkenny
- Laois, T: (057) 866 1800 F: (057) 866
  1800 E: localenterprise@laoiscoco.ie W:
  www.localenterprise.ie/laois
- Leitrim, T: (071) 965 0420 E:
  info@leo.leitrimcoco.ie W:
  www.localenterprise.ie/leitrim
- Limerick, T: (061) 557499 E:
  localenterprise@limerick.ie W:
  www.localenterprise.ie/limerick
- Longford, T: (043) 334 3346 E:
  info@leo.longfordcoco.ie W:
  www.localenterprise.ie/longford
- Louth, T: (1890) 202303 E:
  info@leo.louthcoco.ie W:
  www.localenterprise.ie / louth
- Mayo, T: (094) 904 7555 E:

info@leo.mayococo.ie W: www.localenterprise.ie/mayo
- Meath, Navan Enterprise Centre, Trim Road, Navan, Co Meath T: (046) 907 8400 E: localenterprise@meathcoco.ie W: www.localenterprise.ie/meath
- Monaghan, T: (047) 71818 E: info@leo.monaghancoco.ie W: www.localenterprise.ie/monaghan
- Offaly, T: (057) 935 7480 E: info@leo.offalycoco.ie W: www.localenterprise.ie/offaly
- Roscommon, T: (090) 662 6263 E: localenterprise@roscommoncoco.ie W: www.localenterprise.ie/roscommon
- Sligo, T: (071) 914 4779 E: localenterprise@sligococo.ie W: www.localenterprise.ie/sligo
- South Cork, T: (021) 497 5281 E: southcork@leo.corkcoco.ie W: www.localenterprise.ie/southcork
- Tipperary, T: (052) 612 9466 / 618 7070 E: leo@tipperarycoco.ie W: www.localenterprise.ie/tipperary
- Waterford, T: (0761) 102905 E: info@leo.waterfordcouncil.ie W: www.localenterprise.ie/waterford
- Westmeath, T: (044) 933 8945 E: localenterprise@westmeathcoco.ie W: www.localenterprise.ie/westmeath
- Wexford, T: (053) 919 6020 E: info@leo.wexfordcoco.ie W: www.localenterprise.ie/wexford
- Wicklow, T: (0404) 30800 E: enterprise@wicklowcoco.ie W: www.localenterprise.ie/wicklow

Letterkenny Institute of Technology, Port Road, Letterkenny, Co Donegal F92 FC93 T: (074) 918 6000 E: reception@lyit.ie W: www.lyit.ie

Limerick Enterprise Development Partnership Ltd, Roxboro Road, Limerick T: (061) 469060 E: info@ledp.ie W: www.ledp.ie

Limerick Institute of Technology, Moylish Park, Limerick T: (061) 293000 E: information@lit.ie W: www.lit.ie

Longford Community Resources Ltd, Longford Community Enterprise Centre, Templemichael, Ballinalee Road, Longford N39 T9Y1 T: (043)

334 5555 E: enquiries@ lcrl.ie W: www.lcrl.ie

Louth Leader Partnership, Mayoralty Street, Drogheda, Co Louth T: (041) 984 2088 W: www.louthleaderpartnership.ie

MAC (National Microelectronics Application Centre), Suparule House, Lonsdale Road, Plassey Technology Park, Limerick T: (061) 334699 E: info@mac.ie W: www.mac.ie

Marine Institute, Rinville, Oranmore, Co Galway H91 R673 T: (091) 387200 E: institute.mail@marine.ie W: www.marine.ie

Mayo North East, Lower Main Street, Foxford, Co Mayo T: (094) 925 6745 E: info@mayonortheast.com W: www.mayonortheast.com

Midland Innovation & Research Centre (MIRC), Athlone Institute of Technology, Dublin Road, Athlone, Co Westmeath T: (0906) 471 882 E: mirc@ait.ie W: www.mirc.ie

Monaghan Integrated Development, Monaghan Road, Castleblaney, Co Monaghan T: (042) 974 9500 E: info@monaghanintegrateddevelopment.ie W: www.midl.ie

National Association of Building Co-operatives Ltd, 33 Lower Baggot Street, Dublin 2 T: (01) 661 2877 E: admin@cooperativehousing.ie W: www.cooperativehousing.ie

National Microelectronics Application Centre, See MAC

National Software Centre, NSC Campus, Mahon, Cork T: (021) 230 7000 E: info@nsc-campus.com W: www.nsc-campus.com

National Standards Authority of Ireland, 1 Swift Square, Northwood, Santry, Dublin D09 A0E4 T: (01) 807 3800 E: info@nsai.ie W: www.nsai.ie

National University of Ireland Galway, Galway H91 TK33 T: (091) 524411 E: info@nuigalway.ie W: www.nuigalway.ie

North, East & West Kerry Dvelopment, Aras an Phobail, Croílár na

Mistéalach, Tralee, Co Kerry T: (066) 718 0190 E: seamusohara@nekd.ie W: www.nekd.net

Northern & Western Regional Assembly, The Square, Ballaghaderreen, Co Roscommon T: (094) 986 2970 E: info@bmwassembly.ie W: www.bmwassembly.ie

Northside Partnership, Coolock Development Centre, Bunratty Drive, Coolock, Dublin 17 T: (01) 848 5630 E: info@northsidepartnership.ie W: www.northsidepartnership.ie

Nova UCD, Belfield Innovation Park, University College Dublin, Belfield, Dublin 4 T: (01) 716 3700 E: innovation@ucd.ie W: http://www.ucd.ie/innovation/

Oak Tree Press, 33 Rochestown Rise, Rochestown, Cork T12 EVT0 T: (086) 244 1633 E: brian.okane@oaktreepress.com W: www.oaktreepress.com / www.successstore.com

Offaly Local Development Company, Millennium House, Main Street, Tullamore, Co Offaly T: (057) 935 2467 / 932 2850 E: info@offalyldc.ie W: www.offalyldc.ie

Partas, Bolbrook Enterprise Centre, Avonmore Road, Tallaght, Dublin D24 K07Y T: (01) 414 5700 W: www.partas.ie C: Yvonne Cusack, Enterprise Officer

Patents Office, Government Buildings, Hebron Road, Kilkenny R95 H4XC T: (056) 772 0111 E: patlib@patentsoffice.ie W: www.patentsoffice.ie

PAUL Partnership Limerick, Unit 25a, Tait Business Centre, Dominic Street, Limerick T: (061) 419388 E: info@paulpartnership.ie W: www.paulpartnership.ie

permanent tsb, 56-59 St Stephen's Green, Dublin 2 T: (01) 212 4101 W: www.permanenttsb.ie

PLATO Dublin, The Guinness Enterprise Centre, Taylor's Lane, Dublin 8 T: (086) 823 4309 E: dublin@plato.ie W: www.plato.ie

Pobal, Holbrook House, Holles Street, Dublin 2 T: (01) 511 7000 E: enquiries@pobal.ie W: www.pobal.ie

Rabobank, 2 George's Dock, IFSC, Dublin D01 H2T6, T: (01) 607 6100 W: www.rabobank.ie

Regional Development Centre, Dundalk Institute of Technology, Dublin Road, Dundalk T: (042) 937 0400 E: info@rdc.ie W: www.rdc.ie

Registry of Business Names, Bloom House, Gloucester Place Lower, Dublin 1 T: (01) 804 5200 W: www.cro.ie

Registry of Friendly Societies, Bloom House, Gloucester Place Lower, Dublin 1 T: (01) 804 5200 E: rfs@djei.ie

Revenue Commissioners, Dublin Castle, Dublin 2 W: www.revenue.ie

Roscommon LEADER Partnership, Unit 12, Tower B, Roscommon West Business Park, Golf Links Road, Roscommon Town, Co Roscommon T: (090) 663 0252 E: info@rosleaderpartnership.ie W: www.rosleaderpartnership.ie

Rubicon Centre, CIT Campus, Bishopstown, Cork T: (021) 492 8900 E: paul.healy@rubiconcentre.ie W: www.rubiconcentre.ie

SECAD (South & East Cork Area Development), Owennacurra Business Park, Knockgriffin, Midleton, Co Cork T: (021) 461 3432 E: info@secad.ie W: www.secad.ie

Shannon Commercial Properties, Universal House, One Airport Avenue, Shannon Free Zone, Co Clare T: (061) 710 000 W: www.shannonproperties.ie

Sligo LEADER Partnership Company Ltd, Sligo Development Centre, Cleveragh Road, Sligo T: (071) 914 1138 E: info@sligoleader.com W: www.sligoleader.com

Small Firms Association, Confederation House, 84–86 Lower Baggot Street, Dublin 2 T: (01) 605 1500 F: (01) 638 1668 E: info@sfa.ie W: www.sfa.ie

SOLAS — Further Education and Training Authority, Castleforbes House,

Castleforbes Road, Dublin 1 T: (01) 533 2500 E: info@solas.ie W: www.solas.ie

South Dublin County Partnership, County Hall, Block 3, Belgard Square North, Tallaght, Dublin 24 T: (01) 464 9300 E: info@sdcpartnership.ie W: www.sdcpartnership.ie

South East Business Innovation Centre, Unit 1B, Industrial Park, Cork Road, Waterford T: (051) 356300 E: info@southeastbic.ie W: www.southeastbic.ie

South Kerry Development Partnership Ltd, West Main Street, Caherciveen, Co Kerry T: (066) 947 2724 E: info@skdp.net W: www.southkerry.ie

Southern & Eastern Regional Assembly, Assembly House, O'Connell Street, Waterford X91 F8PC T: (051) 860700 E: info@southernassembly.ie W: www.southernassembly.ie

Southside Partnership Ltd, The Old Post Office, 7 Rock Hill, Main Street, Blackrock, Co Dublin T: (01) 706 0100 W: www.southsidepartnership.ie

SPADE Enterprise Centre, North King Street, Dublin 7 T: (01) 617 4800 W: www.spade.ie

Teagasc — The Agriculture Food and Development Authority, Oak Park, Carlow R93 XE12 T: (059) 917 0200 F: (059) 918 2097 E: info@teagasc.ie W: www.teagasc.ie

Terenure Enterprise Centre, 17 Rathfarnham Road, Terenure, Dublin 6W T: (01) 490 3237 F: (01) 490 3238 E: mhannon@terenure-enterprise.ie W: www.terenure-enterprise.ie

The LINC, Institute of Technology Blanchardstown, Blanchardstown Road North, Blanchardstown, Dublin 15 T: (01) 885 1502 E : claire.macnamee@itb.ie W: http://www.itb.ie/IndustryInnovation/thelinc.html

Tyndall National Institute, Lee Maltings, Dyke Parade, Cork T12 R5CP T: (021) 234 6177 E: info@tyndall.ie W: www.tyndall.ie

Údarás na Gaeltachta, Na Forbacha, Gaillimh T: (091) 503100 E: eolas@udaras.ie W: www.udaras.ie

Ulster Bank, George's Quay, Dublin D02 VR98 W: www. ulsterbank.ie

University College Cork, Cork T: (021) 490 3000 W: www.ucc.ie

University College Dublin, Belfield, Dublin 4 T: (01) 716 7777 E: cody.mayoh@ucd.ie W: www.ucd.ie

University of Dublin, Trinity College, College Green, Dublin 2 T: (01) 896 1000 W: www.tcd.ie

University of Limerick, Plassey, Limerick V94 T9PX T: (061) 202700 W: www.ul.ie

Waterford Area Partnership, Westgate Park, Tramore Road, Waterford T: (051) 841740 E: info@wap.ie W: www.wap.ie

Waterford Institute of Technology, Cork Road, Waterford T: (051) 302000 E: info@wit.ie W: www.wit.ie

Waterford LEADER Partnership Ltd, Lismore Business Park, Lismore, Co Waterford T: (058) 54646 E: info@wlp.ie W: www.wlp.ie

West Limerick Resources Ltd, St. Mary's Road, Newcastlewest, Co Limerick T: (069) 62222 E: info@wlr.ie W: www.wlr.ie

WestBIC, Galway Technology Centre, Mervue, Galway T: (091) 730 850 E: info@westbic.ie W: www. westbic.ie

Westmeath Community Development Ltd, Mullingar ETI Centre, Mullingar Business Park, Mullingar, Co Westmeath N91 X012 T: (044) 934 8571 W: www.westcd.ie

Wexford Local Development, Spawell Road, Wexford T: (053) 915 5800 E: info@wld.ie W: www.wld.ie

OAK TREE PRESS

Oak Tree Press develops and delivers information, advice and resources for entrepreneurs and managers. It is Ireland's leading business book publisher, with an unrivalled reputation for quality titles across business, management, human resources, law, marketing and enterprise topics.

In addition, Oak Tree Press occupies a unique position in start-up and small business support in Ireland through its standard-setting titles, as well as training courses, mentoring and advisory services.

Oak Tree Press is comfortable across a range of communication media – print, web and training, focusing always on the effective communication of business information.

OAK TREE PRESS

33 Rochestown Rise, Cork, Ireland.
T: + 353 86 244 1633 / + 353 86 330 7694
E: info@oaktreepress.com W: www.oaktreepress.com.